MELVA B. ROBERTSON

Congratulations!

IT'S A BRAND

The entrepreneur's guide to birthing the
brand, identifying the target audience, and
increasing visibility

Booking and Purchasing Information:
Contact: The Write Media Group, PR
info@thewritemediagrp.com
www.thewritemediagrp.com
Melva Robertson: melvarobertson@gmail.com

Book Editor: Karen McCollum Rodgers
Cover Design: Ana Grigoriu
Photography: Brian Pride Photography
Foreword: Michael Smart – Michael Smart PR
Cover model: Mikah K. Berrien

Dedication:

This book is dedicated to my life's greatest influences: God, my husband, Min. Dereko J. Robertson; my amazing daughter Miss Aria Jayde Robertson; and my mother, Dr. Florence J. Bell. I would like to also dedicate this book to my greatest supporters, my family, Hilda Walker, Ricky and Benita Reed, Lila Robertson, Brandon and Jordan Robertson, and Nancy Sargent. A special thank you is also in order for my wonderful colleague Heather Slaughter; you have been a Godsend.

To my innumerable support system of family, friends, and colleagues I thank you from the bottom of my heart for always being the positive voices of encouragement, love, prayers, and motivation. I possess the courage to follow my dreams because of you all.

In memory of Deward and Hazel Jackson and Olivia Bell

Table of Contents:

Foreword

To the reader: I respect you so much.

Because you're an entrepreneur. You took action. You *started*. And now you're digging deeper to strengthen your expertise and grow your business.

Most of us entrepreneurs get distracted by operations. We worry about fulfillment and how we're going to respond to customers. But none of that matters if we don't get the brand right and actually attract the customers. And too often marketing advice ignores the power of public relations.

That's the secret weapon you're holding in your hand – rare insight into ways you can take advantage of free publicity and third-party credibility to earn that rarest of business assets: the trust of the people in your core audience.

Think of how often businesses let you down. How many actually do what they say they'll do? When you simply act consistently with your marketing, your customers start to trust you with their business. Then they trust you with their friends.

Plenty of marketers talk about this, but most of them think only in terms of paid advertising and collateral. Melva is going to introduce you to PR principles which, when applied correctly, achieve even better results than those old standbys.

Now, to borrow the parlance of this book's title, you need to start with "baby" steps. PR strategies and tactics will blow up in your face if you don't first establish the foundations that Melva will walk you through in the beginning chapters. Once you master those, you'll be ready for the social media and PR tips she saves for last.

Congratulations on being a go-getter. I wish you all the success in the world.

Michael Smart

CEO, MichaelSMARTPR

Introduction:

Whate exactly is it that you do?

Congratulations! It's a...Brand! As you read this, I hear you saying to me, "Melva, what are you talking about?" Well, I'm glad you asked that question. When clients or potential clients come to me they often refer to their businesses as their babies. You may have even done this yourself. If they don't have children, the business is their baby. If they do have children, the business is still their baby. As a mother and a business owner, I can definitely understand the thought of your business, product, service, or brand feeling like your child. It all started with a vision or idea (the conception). Then as you continued thinking about it, you took the time to write down your ideas, and brainstorm ways to make this vision work for you. You've attended conferences and seminars, you read books such as this one, did the groundwork and made the necessary steps to start your business (the pregnancy). Finally, whether it was one month, nine months or nine years later, you began functioning as a legitimate business (the birth). So as I stated before, congratulations, it's a brand and if you aren't a brand yet, well, by the time you finish this book, I will be able to offer my congrats again!

A question commonly posed to me is this: "Now what exactly is it that you do?" I can't tell you how many times I hear this question. In fact, I really wish I had a dollar for every time someone asks me this. Even in the corporate setting during my full-time public relations positions, I was asked by other departments or colleagues, "What is it that you do?" This is a question that my mother has asked; other family members and friends have asked; and let's face it...a lot of people have asked. Just recently a social media "friend" reached out to me privately and said, I've seen you with this person and that person, and here and there (I'm paraphrasing here); if you don't mind my asking, what exactly do you do? All I could do was laugh. So I figured why not begin this book with the answer to that question so we can move forward.

The very reason that I am writing this book is to help entrepreneurs develop the roadmap to efficiently build their brands. The word brand is often tossed around inaccurately, which causes the unsuspecting entrepreneur to focus heavily on branding aspects that they perceive to be important. In the meantime the true core of branding goes untouched, resulting in the opposite of what you hoped for—an under-developed brand. I don't want anyone spending the time, energy, or resources developing something or focused on something that is not accurately related to the core of their brand or brand identity.

This book is designed to help entrepreneurs understand the foundational strategies that will be beneficial to their future growth, development and expansion as a business and a brand. Ultimately the strategies outlined in this book will lay a foundation for increased visibility, create and build relationships with potential clients, partnerships and media outlets, and achieve overall clear communication to the masses of your organization's purpose and abilities. That's the role of public relations and that, in a simplified nutshell, is what we public relations professionals strive to help our clients achieve.

I won't get too technical, because all of that comes later in the upcoming chapters, but I will say that basically I, as a public relations professional, communicate for my clients in some cases and in others I help my clients figure out the best way to communicate for themselves. That's a pretty broad explanation, I know, but if we start there everything else that I say later on will make sense. In terms of public relations or hiring a publicist, think of the communication element. Our job is to help you communicate as well as to manage the information that goes from your brand to your audience.

Determining exactly what to say to make people "get it" about your brand is not an easy task. It takes a concerted effort to think of ways to tailor your message in a way that is clear, accurate, and sustainable. A publicist can help you connect this important piece of your branding puzzle. Even if you don't have an ongoing agreement with a publicist, the counsel of a public relations expert in the beginning phases of your brand development eliminates the potential for miscommunication or the need to rebrand down the line. Successful businesses have effective brands. The right branding strategy can place your product or service in the forefront of your industry.

Have you ever wanted to say something, but you just didn't know the right words to use to say it? You may call a friend and say something such as, "What's the best way to say I'm mad without saying, 'I'm mad'?" Your friend, who is most likely the one you called because he or she is either in the communications business or may just be a wordsmith, might reply, "You should say, I am concerned about the direction this situation is taking." Ah ha! That's it. That's what you really wanted to say. Your friend helped you figure out a way to communicate what you wanted to say in a way that hopefully doesn't cause additional conflict and will perhaps provide a line to resolution and clear interpretation. Well that my friend, is public relations.

We help companies, entrepreneurs or brands identify the best way to communicate their messages to their target audiences. We take it a step further; however, by also looking at how to say basically the same thing in a way that is understandable to different types of audiences. This could happen by connecting our clients to potential partners, building a communications campaign targeted at specific audiences, or generating media attention. Then we try to identify the best way to get that message to each audience. We want the right people to know you and to like you or your brand; so we help build relationships with key players in order to create one big happy family that communicates.

The other component to this PR puzzle is the unpleasant one. There may come a time when unfortunately everyone won't like you or they fall out of love with you and at that point, we rush in to figure out the best way to mend that broken relationship and move forward past the "incident." We call that crisis communications. Crisis communications is basically managing the unexpected as it relates to your perception or image. We, the public relations experts, are the ones who help put out the "reputation" fires in your business. We then develop more strategies to rebuild your audience's trust. As I mentioned before, you will understand the specifics of the role of a publicist, the function and need for public relations strategies and the difference between PR and marketing.

I have worked in public relations for 15 years. I earned my Bachelor of Arts degree in Mass Communications from Morris Brown College, a private college in Atlanta,

Georgia and my Master of Arts degree in professional writing from Kennesaw State University. Both institutions, along with my experience since receiving my bachelor's degree, have provided indescribable experiences in this field. When I started my undergrad, I had aspirations of becoming a broadcast television reporter. After a few internships at several news stations in Atlanta and freelance reporting jobs for about eight months after graduation, I felt less enthusiastic about reporting, but I still loved the media environment. While freelancing I was also working full time for one of the largest public health systems in the southeast. I can't really say whether it was exhaustion or fate, but I decided I no longer wanted to pursue reporting and I would rather continue my pursuit of becoming a public relations professional. Thirteen years later after a successful stint in corporate communications, in addition to working at one of the top 10 universities in the nation, I decided to start my own PR company. From there as the clients rolled in and opportunities presented themselves, what began as a part time "side job" has now morphed into a fully functional boutique PR and writing services firm.

Between my combined 15 years of experience, the hard-hitting, no-holds-barred experiences as an entrepreneur, and watching the ups and downs of my clients' experiences, I have learned quite a bit that I would like to share with you in this book. I designed this book as a branding and PR 101 guide for start-up companies, individuals, and emerging entrepreneurs. Whether you have a personal brand, corporate brand or something in between, I will define some generally tossed around concepts you may not understand, but should definitely become familiar with on your journey to entrepreneurial success. Most importantly, I will present the idea of branding to you in a way that I think will help eliminate some of the pitfalls that I see constantly in this business.

Chapter 1: **The Branding Principle**

"**I** need help building my brand."

"I'm really working on my brand right now and have some exciting things coming up this year."

"We are doing a total rebrand for the business and it's going to be great!"

"My brand! My brand! My brand!"

I hear these and a few other branding references all of the time. Everyone seems to understand that branding is important; they just don't fully understand what branding encompasses. They may not really even understand why branding is so important. I guess the great part is that entrepreneurs pay attention when I mention the word brand, even if they are not sure about the true definition. The challenge is that I later find that branding in its true definition is not what some expected it to be. My introduction to the potential client's brand sometimes begins with a lengthy explanation about the graphic designer for their logo or the business cards that he or she ordered.

When I dig deeper, I learn that the individual may not have put enough thought into the characteristics of the brand.   This revelation leads to a meeting where I educate the client on basic strategic requirements. Quite naturally, when thinking of "the brand," people automatically think of websites, business cards, logos and colors. They even think of the product itself.   These references are not entirely erroneous; those are concepts of branding, but a true brand is much more than that.

Branding in a nutshell is your product's identity. It's an image. Think about that for a moment: It's an image; better yet, it is a reputation. Your brand is the reputation of whatever you are selling. If you don't quite get it yet, that's ok; we will go deeper into these concepts in the upcoming chapters, but branding is how you want people to see your product or service. The logo, website, and all of those other components support that identity, but they aren't the true identity. Branding is how you want people to think and feel when they hear about your product. The problem with branding; however, is that although it involves how we *want* people to identify us, branding problems come along when what we portray is not what is actually experienced.

Let's dig a little deeper into this. First, let me add this disclaimer: I am from the South! I come from southern hospitability, sweet tea, grits, and words such as "y'all" and "fixin' to." If you don't know what I'm talking about, here is a translation for some of my non-southern readers. If I say, "Thank y'all for taking the time to read this book," that really means, "Thank **you, everyone** for reading this book." If I say, "I'm fixin' to fix breakfast," that means, "I am about to prepare breakfast." Got it? Ok, just a little pause from Branding 101 to touch on Southern Lingo 101.

So now, about the South: In the South, specifically Atlanta, Georgia, we have a few things: the 1996 Olympics, big yards, "y'all" as I mentioned earlier and Chick-fil-A. In my world, everyone should know about Chick-fil-A, but I do realize that everyone doesn't, so let me explain why we are even talking about this. Chick-fil-

A started out as a family owned business founded by S. Truett Cathy. Mr. Cathy had a reputation for morals, family, religion, and business.

There is a long history behind it that I won't bother going into here, but the main point to remember is the restaurant was and still is family owned and oriented, Christian-based, and founded on hospitality and values. To this day, lines are wrapped around Chick-fil-A pretty much from open to close because the food is good and the customer service is even better. People trust the Chick-fil-A brand to be who they say they are; and that's exactly what you also should desire for your brand.

Chick-fil-A's brand is mainly that of the family's reputation. The Cathys are very community and youth oriented, innovative, faith-based, and ethical. No matter which Chick-fil-A you enter, you will get the same level of customer service that keeps you wanting to return. You will be greeted with a smile, you will find that most of the employees are young people, (largely due to their emphasis on educational opportunities through employment), and the food will be outstanding. I could write another separate chapter on the lemonade itself, but I will stay on topic.

The restaurant is not open on Sundays or holidays. Since the beginning the founder of Chick-fil-A has operated the restaurant under a strict "closed-on Sundays" policy. Due to their belief in family and their faith, Mr. Cathy wanted the employees to be able to spend time with their families on these special days throughout the year. So he closed the stores on these days and the magical part about it is the company has not seen a profit loss yet from that decision.

Chick-fil-A is the branding prototype because everything that the brand portrays is what customers experience. I could go on and on about Chick-fil-A, but the reason for mentioning it is because the brand (what is portrayed) matches the perception (what is actually viewed). So if you are in the South or the newer locations outside of the southern states, you can ask anyone about Chick-fil-A. You will hear the same types of descriptions: superb customer service, clean facilities, great food, healthy options, focus on family, etc. All of these descriptions line up with what is portrayed and that is good branding.

Let me emphasize a term that is extremely important: Brand alignment. Notice that I mentioned how the public perception of Chick-fil-A aligned with the company's brand? That's imperative for your brand as well. **Your actions and image should align.** This is especially true for those with personal brands. People will quickly dismiss your brand if you are found to contradict who you say you are. Branding all boils down to trust. Your audience will not support you if they do not feel that they can trust you.

Consider this, if you are a community activist with a platform revolved around justice for all, women's rights, equality, etc. and you are "caught" saying or doing something that does not align with that image, you are no longer trustworthy in the eyes of your clients. The next few months plus of your career will be spent "fixing" your PR issue. Quite frankly, people are turned off by disloyalty and as with any relationship, trust that is broken is a challenge to rebuild. It's much harder to rebuild an image than it is to maintain one. Consciously focusing on your brand alignment will help you to stay focused on the objective of your brand.

In the cases of brands such as Chick-fil-A, the community service projects that they support align with their community advocacy reputation. Simply put, they say that they care about the community and they have projects and initiatives to support that claim. They also value youth development and family, so they align that claim with youth-focused initiatives that provide scholarships for college bound students, and family focused initiatives both community wide and storewide, that all align with the brand. A company must be able to prove that they are who they claim to be and aligned initiatives and projects are the best ways to ensure a sustainable and thriving brand.

An effective brand does a few things. It helps to establish sustainability, trust, growth, and of course profit. Today, according to the company's website, Chick-fil-A is the second largest quick-service chicken restaurant chain in the country. It has more than 1900 stores in 42 states and for the past 47 consecutive years, it has experienced an annual sales increase. That is impressive. What's more impressive is that remember, this company has experienced these types of numbers while only operating six days out of the week rather than seven. Staying true to its identity or brand plays an instrumental part of its success.

Now let's take a look at a few other examples. Coca-Cola (another Atlanta invention) is a brand that falls in line with its mission to refresh the world, create value and make a difference. Although they have evolved throughout the years, their physical appearance has not changed much. The newer products and brands have stayed consistent with the mission and every initiative, whether community service, sponsorship, or partnership, is aligned with the brand's mission. The success story of this company is that today the Coca-Cola Company, through its assortment of beverages, has over 500 beverage brands sold in more than 200 countries. The business results seem to align with its mission for global outreach, values, consistency, and creativity.

I remember being highly impressed with Coca-Cola a few years ago when I reached out to them with a sponsorship request for an event. It goes without saying that all companies are selective when it comes to donations, but I was really impressed and proud of the emphasis communicated by Coke on the mandatory alignment between the event in question and Coke's initiatives. In other words they aren't endorsing anything that does not align with their brand. I respect that because it shows that they are aware of the value of their brand. Even though a cause may be "worthy," you must be selective in your brand's associations.

Your brand is your reputation. No matter how enticing some opportunities may seem, if they do not align with your brand, walk away. At this point in the book you may or may not know exactly what your brand is and we will deal that, but understand that after you have defined your brand, everything else must align with that definition. As a new or emerging entrepreneur, it can be exciting to join forces with whoever may request to work with you. You can think of it as exposure, networking, or new opportunities and in most cases it may be, but if it turns out that their brand doesn't align with yours, or there is any conflict in your collaboration with what you have communicated to your audience, you should decline the opportunity.

I have clients who receive requests that sound like great opportunities but before we decide, we carefully research the company, its past events or other collaborations, past affiliations, and the potential company's overall brand. Is that too much? Not at all! That is exactly what you should do before doing anything related to your business. Make sure that your brand, goals, and mission mesh. Follow Coke's lead and develop a selection process with a list of questions and criteria that you will follow before accepting these types of requests.

And then there is Apple. Their logo is an apple; the name is apple. That sounds simple enough, but it is so much more complex; Apple is listed number one on Forbes World's Most Valuable Brands list totaling $145.3 billion in brand value. When you think of Apple you tend to have confidence in the product. We, the consumers, identify with its innovation and leadership in technology. We also recognize and reconcile that an Apple product will come with a hefty price tag. It seems as though no one minds; however, judging by the obscenely long lines wrapped around the buildings on the night before a new release. Consumers also understand that although the product will come with a hefty price tag, there is longevity and security in that product as well. That's called trust. There is that word again! People believe in the brand because the brand has proven to be what it has proclaimed that it will be. For that reason, even after the latest Apple product has been released, there is anticipation and excitement for the next product because the brand has proven to be effective.

That brings me to another point. When your brand is trusted and proven, customers don't mind paying for it. They feel that it is worth the price. They trust that there will be some type of return on the investment. Think about all the high end products, services, restaurants, clothes, shoes, accessories, and businesses that exist. Based on branding alone, some of those associated price tags are never questioned. We expect the price to be steep and are even shocked if there is a sale or discount provided. Some brands are even known for never having sales or discounts and as customers; we respect and accept it (judging by the lines wrapped around the buildings when a new Apple product is released) it, because we know the value of that brand.

Now that you've seen a few examples, let's apply these principles to your brand. What do you want to be known for? Yes, you may be a great cook and your restaurant may serve the same menu as all of the other restaurants out there, but what else do you want to be associated with? As a restaurant owner an automatic default is to have great food and great service; so now in addition to that, what else will be your reputation? This is not a question you should rush to answer, because this question will be one of the defining pieces to your brand development. Throughout this book, really ponder how all of the principles you will learn, fall back to the answer to this question. Don't let your brand break its promise to your customers because you didn't give the appropriate consideration to what you can really deliver. Be truthful and honest with yourself first, about your brand and then tailor everything from the name of your business to your mission statement to that promise.

I want you to notice that when discussing the brands above, I have not mentioned anything about the effectiveness of their logos, or what type of font they used, or even their colors or slogans. Yes, they all have recognizable logos and pretty unique names, but that is not what makes people utilize them. I simply discussed their reputation, their identity.   These brands are consistent with who the business says that they are and how they actually operate; and because of this alone, people believe in the brand and recognize its value.

Ladies and gentleman, that is what branding is all about. The name is not the brand; the logo is not the brand; the brand is the actual quality of service that you provide to your target client, aligned with the actual quality of service that they receive. It's simple; no matter what your niche is—whether you are a motivational speaker and you are the brand, or you have a product, or maybe you are a plumber or writer—you want to put out an identity that you can actually deliver.

Think about this...your name may be Mary; but so are countless others. What makes you (Mary) stand out from all of the other Marys out there? It's your personality. Better yet, it's your reputation. You (Mary) may be kind and generous, whereas another "Mary" may be selfish and rude. Although the "other Mary" may claim to be kind and generous, if she does not actually deliver kindness and generosity, then her reputation or brand is ineffective and fallible. On the other hand, if you (Mary) are actually kind and generous and that's how people see you, then you have an effective brand or reputation, because what you portray matches what you actually do.

I use the example of names because so many times when entrepreneurs first have a business idea, they spend so much time focusing on a clever name and logo. All of that truly is important; yes, but equally, if not more importantly, you must make sure you can develop a brand you can actually deliver. If my brand is that my product is all natural or organic, then I must make sure that consistently, even when it is easier or less costly to produce non-organic foods, I must remain true to my brand.

You understand that when the brand that is portrayed is not consistent with what the client experiences, the brand becomes untrustworthy. You will find that companies embark on rebranding for several reasons. It could be that their brand is outdated because it has changed so much from when the company originally started. The company wants to head in a new direction or maybe the new leadership has a new vision for the company. Rebranding isn't necessarily a bad thing, when you choose to rebrand and are not forced to rebrand. I've found; however, that the companies that have not had to rebrand usually have that longevity because they took the time in the beginning to analyze who they were and how they wanted to operate.

If you rush through the branding process, you may find yourself having to rebrand sooner rather than later. Don't worry, there are people out there (present company included) who can train and educate you and work with you on ways to make sure that your branding stays consistent. We will talk about this more later, but components such as public relations, and marketing all support branding efforts and working with the right people through this process helps to ensure that you are on the right path to a sustainable and effective brand.

When I consult with people about their business, the first thing I do is ask them to tell me about the company, then I ask, "Tell me about your brand." Sometimes I get strange looks because people are not really sure how to answer that question, but my asking it is intentional. I want to find out if the person can really communicate who they are and why I need their service. If they can answer the question with no problem or at least with a general idea, then I know that we are ready to really dive into the reputation that we will try to establish for the company. Thinking of the reputation, you may say, well I want my company to be known as a "good company with services that will get results." Well don't we all! We have to dig deeper when talking about the brand and as we venture into the next chapter, I will help you really think about how to **stand out and create an identity** that is unique to your business no matter how many other businesses are out there like yours.

Before going into the next chapter, let's do a quick recap. The brand is the image or reputation. Take the time to really think about "who" your business is. This can be difficult to do because at times it is hard for us, as individuals to really understand who *we* are, let alone our business. The truth is that you must know both, because you and your business, as you will learn, will go hand in hand.

Chapter 2: **It's Time to Conceive**

At the time of this writing, I am the mother of a loveable little four-year-old girl. As a first time mom there have been so many things that I've learned about myself, my husband, my body, my emotions, my beliefs, my intellect, my work ethic, my abilities...whew, the list goes on and on about my lessons learned. Notice that I have not yet even mentioned actually learning about my child. Before she even arrived, I started learning about myself and the characteristics mentioned above. Let me just tell you from one parent to another, all of those things changed constantly before she even graced this world with her beautiful presence.

I hear you again saying, "Why are you telling us this, Melva?" I'm telling you this because I imagine that like me, you are going through all types of emotional ups and downs when it comes to how to start your business; how to grow your business; the next step for your business; how to increase visibility for your business, who to add to your business, etc. Whether you are male or female, you are pondering the very natural and realistic concerns of anyone embarking on a journey that will forever change their lives. So in this chapter, I am going to talk to you from one parent to another because whether you realize it or not, you are now a parent and we all know that there was a process of conception, pregnancy, and birth that you had to experience before you achieved this great title of parent.

The conception!

We all learned about the birds and the bees, probably earlier in life than necessary so I won't give you that lesson (thank me later). But just as a child is conceived, so is your business. The ideas and vision you have about starting your business or pursuing your career are the conception of that business. It's the fertilization of something that you will later birth and something that you will have a first-hand opportunity to develop and grow.

During conception, you realized that you wanted to start this business. You realized that your "baby" is needed and belongs in this world. As with any parent, you began to envision the different stages of the growth of your business, such as your opening day, the look of your website, your potential clients and of course, your great world domination! You started thinking of business names and writing them down to see how they look on paper. You imagined your commercials and billboards and all of the speaking engagements and media interviews you would garner.

I recall my husband and me going back and forth on names for our child so often that I thought she might have about four or five names when all was said and done. The excitement and anticipation of all of the possibilities was almost overwhelming and we had to have just the right name to match everything that we hoped and dreamed for her. I'll talk specifically about that later but I'm sure you get my point here. When you are conceiving your business, you dream of limitless possibilities. Your mind takes you to so many places, and without sounding completely cheesy, you feel as though you can have it all.

Conception is an important step in your business; it's actually the most important phase because without it, there really is no business. How can you lead a company if you have no vision for it? How can you motivate your employees or sell your business to potential investors and clients if you can't see past year one? The short answer is that you can't. This is why out of all of the time that you spend on your business development, conception should receive the most thought. So let's talk about three key components in the conception of your business.

1. **Not even the sky is the limit.** This is my favorite part of the branding/business process because it is uninhibited. It costs *nothing* to have an idea. Dreams are free! You don't need anyone's help to brainstorm and whatever you come up with in this phase has potential for success. It's uninhibited because there is no rejection in brainstorming, there are no barriers, and there is no pressure because literally all that you have to do is think. You don't need anyone's help to think. Sure later on down the road or maybe even next

week, you can have a brainstorming session with trusted friends and mentors, but your initial thoughts and hopes for your business should be yours. The best thing about that is whatever you come up with has potential. Few things in life are absolutely free but thinking, I can assure you, is one of those things. So think. Think about everything that you want for your business and brand.

When I am conceiving, I like to envision everything from the name, the grand opening, my first customer, my first million, my subsidiaries, retirement, to the family legacy that the business will leave, the future in general, and anything else that my mind can conceive. The ideas are nonstop. This is an important phase, because during conception you have an opportunity to really visualize the future, envision the legacy that your brand will leave, and you can then start to think about the specific characteristics of your brand.

Let me give you an example; before my husband and I conceived Aria (my daughter), we talked about her all the time.   We envisioned her personality; we envisioned vacations and birthday parties, family outings, her likes, her dislikes, her career, the footprint that she would leave in this world. We envisioned pretty much her entire life and beyond in actuality, because we also thought about her grandchildren.   Yes, we did a lot of thinking; but in that thinking, we were able to talk about our role in making our dream for her life a reality. Of course she would have her own dreams and her life would evolve into its own unique sphere, but our vision for her would serve as a starting point or a foundation and along the way we would work together to mold it into success for her.

During that time my husband and I were essentially thinking about our family's brand. How would we raise her? How early would she start school? Would she go to day care? Will she attend public or private school? When will she start dating? What will be her curfew when she is 16?   My husband, being a father, even started thinking—and ultimately pouting—about the day that he would have to walk her down the aisle. Again, that's a lot of thinking about a person who wasn't even conceived yet.

This may sound very anal and obsessive, but truthfully, it's not. We were planning to embark on a life-altering experience for her and for us and we wanted to not only plan and prepare for our family's future, but we also wanted to think about the endless positive possibilities for us all. Naturally, we also thought about some of the negatives and ways that we would prepare for those. We thought about barriers to our parenting versus society's parenting and how to overcome those things. The point I'm trying to make here is that the vision is the only way you will begin to equip yourself for the journey that lies ahead with your business.

I must point out that although you have a plan, the plans will be altered. Just as I mentioned about Aria's life morphing into its own unique form, your business will do the same. There will always be unexpected twists and turns. Some will be positive and some not so much, but the good thing about this phase is that you can lay a foundation that is so solid, you even start preparing for the unexpected. I once worked for a department called Emergency Preparedness and Response and one thing that we believed was that preparation is a response. By thoroughly brainstorming and thinking about the life of your business, you are already steps ahead of the process of finding solutions to those potential barriers. At least you have a plan; preparation is the key to success in anything.

2. **Think Forward.** In case you haven't guessed, I am encouraging you to think past the short-term. Yes, you need a name; yes, you need a website; yes, you definitely need to open for business but beyond that, during day five, week five, decade five, you need a plan. After that you need a back-up plan. The main objective is to plan ahead. Think of possible barriers and think of ways to overcome them. Think of possible triumphs and think of ways to build on them. Preparation is key

and yes, the plans may change along the way but through proper planning you are at least building a model to help keep you focused and prepared for what is to come.

One vital component to our thought process before my daughter arrived was thinking about what type of person we wanted her to become. Please pay attention to this part because this is how you develop your brand. We wanted our daughter to be likeable, compassionate, smart and sociable (among other things) and because of this we started thinking of what we needed to do to give her the foundation for those characteristics. Did you hear that? I said that we determined her image and then we determined how we would make it so.

This is exactly what you do with your brand. As you are thinking, figure out the key characteristics of your company:

- Will your company fill a need that does not exist?
- How will your product make people feel?

- Will your service or product be impeccable compared to the competition's service or product?

If your business is a restaurant, will the customer service, food, and experience surpass the competitor's? If so, how? If you are a designer or retailer, will your clothes have a reputation for their affordable or high end pricing? Depending on which one, how will the quality of your merchandise reflect that? If you provide a service, will that service be known as timely and efficient? Or will it be known as expensive because of the quality and experience of the workers? Maybe it will be known by the type of products that you use to perform your service? Whatever your "thing" is, figure out how to make sure what you want to happen happens.

These are just a few of the things to consider when you are thinking of your brand. There are many questions to ask and none of the answers are wrong; the answers simply define how you operate and how you portray yourself to your audience. The answers to these questions define your brand!

3. **Write it down.** As you are brainstorming, thinking, and envisioning, don't forget to write everything down. The brain can only retain so much and just because you think about it now, does not mean that you will remember it later. As a writer, I cannot tell you how many times I have forgotten a great idea for a book chapter or a catchy slogan for an ad, or even a great title for an event; all because I never took the time to write it down. When you initially think of the idea, it seems so great that you are sure you won't forget it until life happens and guess what—you forget it!

We can't control when we will have a great idea, or what will spark some type of inspiration, I get that; but we can be prepared for those spontaneous moments when they happen. For such occasions, I always keep a notepad around me, even if it is a very small "grocery-list" type of writing pad and in this smartphone society that we live in, we can use the electronic notepad or voice memo to record our ideas when they come. The main point is to get the thoughts out of your head and onto something viewable so that you can review and build on them later.

When you write, your ideas become tangible. In your head, it's just a thought but on paper that idea is one step closer to reality. I was tagged in a post on social media once that said, "Ideas are goals without deadlines," while I understand where the person was going with that statement, I am a strong advocate for putting deadlines on your ideas because that way, they actually happen. I don't want you to just think. I want you to think *and act*; that's how brands grow, partnerships form, and success manifests.

Even if your ideas seem totally ludicrous and off the wall, write them down anyway. I believe that every invention used today was sparked by someone's crazy, off-the-wall idea. Let's think about this in simplified terms: do you really think that back in the early 1800s people actually believed that one day we would not only drive cars, but talk on the phone, watch movies or heaven forbid, have the car talk to us (i.e. navigation systems, etc.). Those things would seem off the wall back then, I'm sure but they are our reality today.

Let's bring it in a little closer. When I was a child, I would not have imagined that today I would be able to actually see a person while talking on the phone or talk on the phone while flying in an airplane. When I was a child we had car phones that didn't leave the car and now, people rarely make the slightest move without their phones because of all the different features available. My grandfather is deceased now, but during his career he was a postal worker. I'm sure that if he were alive today, he would be astonished that email, electronic billing and "downloading" have pretty much taken the place of a good ol' fashioned letter in the mail. My point is that as crazy as it seems right now, there is more than likely a need and a place for your wacky, non-conventional business idea, so think about the possibilities, think even more about the future, and write all of it down.

My last point about the value of writing down your ideas during conception is that your ideas seem less intimidating when you can see them written. Intimidation is a huge factor in why aspiring entrepreneurs stay "aspiring." In your head, your ideas are sharing space with all of the negative thoughts and reasons why they won't work. On paper, the only things that you are writing at this stage are the possibilities and solutions. Negativity is a big bully! I don't know about you but I am totally against bullying. Sign me up for the anti-bullying campaign because bullying is a no-no in my life. I have no tolerance for it, whether it's cyber bullying, social bullying, or those pesky negative thoughts that try to bully the potential right out of your head. Do your ideas a favor and take them out of that negative environment and put them in their own space where they can flourish and grow.

Remember earlier when I said that your thoughts become tangible once they are on paper? Well they also grow when they are on paper. I love writing and one thing that I've learned from my writing experiences is that in my head I may have a cluster of incomplete "bright ideas" but on paper, when I start writing, all of the dots start to connect. In my head, although I had this chapter idea, I had not figured out how I was going to make this chapter fluid and understandable. As soon as I started writing, everything started to connect. The ideas made more sense, the sentences started to flow and the road map started to align. The same thing happens when you write down your ideas. It holds you accountable and it also grows on the page with gaps connected and questions answered.

Let's talk about accountability for a brief moment, shall we? Accountability is what is going to keep you from "starting" your business for the next 10 years and running your business for the past 10 years. What do I mean? You've asked that a lot so far, but I'm ready with the answers! I mean that I have had potential clients come to me seeking branding advice asking questions such as, "How do I start?" "What do I do?" "How do I know when the time is right?" "How do I find the courage to take the next step?"

I always answer with the following questions:

"What is your business?" – If you can't at least tell me the gist of what you do, then you are still having trouble conceiving. Even if you don't have all of the pieces connected, you should be able to solidly communicate the idea for your business. If you can't, that's ok; just know that it may take a few more attempts at trying to conceive. Maybe all of the ideas are not out of your head and down on paper. Maybe you haven't asked yourself some of the questions mentioned earlier or more importantly, answered them so that you know the characteristics of your business and brand. I guarantee you that if you challenge yourself to answer the toughest questions about your business and branding goals, the answers will lead to a clearly defined brand.

"What have you done?" - This is important because it lets me know where you are in the birthing process and it should make you feel accountable for working a little harder to conceive. Couples who have a hard time conceiving a child try so many different tactics to get pregnant. I have friends who desperately wanted a baby so they did what was medically necessary to make that happen, whether it was healthier living, medical procedures, or just patience. Whatever the case, the need to have their child was so great that they were willing to work hard to make it happen.

The same goes for truly motivated entrepreneurs; they tirelessly search for ways to birth their visions. It is so inspiring when I know of a couple who can't conceive a child and they begin sharing all of the efforts that that are putting forth to make it happen. This is the same drive and determination that you must have when conceiving your business. The questions that I ask are questions that you can ask yourself to help you remain accountable to your goals. You aren't on anyone's specific timeline but you will certainly never meet the deadline if you don't take the proper actions to finally birth your brand. There are no excuses in this process. Just as I tell my daughter, "can't" is not in our vocabularies. The same goes for you. There is always a way and the only one with the power to stop you is you!

"What's wrong with right now?" This is my answer to the "When is the right time to start?" question. Just as with planning for a child, there is never a perfect time. There is never enough money, never enough time, and never a perfect circumstance to bring the child into and the same goes for starting a business. **My thought is that whenever the passion to conceive is so persistent that you feel incomplete unless you start it, you are ready to start.** Starting holds you accountable because once you start, you feel compelled to see an end result. So in the words of Nike, Inc. Just do it! I'll conclude the book with more about getting started, but let me just say this, **if you NEVER start, it will never happen; if you always delay, you will always be behind.** There is no time like the present.

I believe that of all the steps we've discussed so far, writing down your ideas is really the beginning of fertilization. The business start-up process can truly begin when you write down your ideas. In fact, even if you have already started your business, the best way for it to continue is the same: write everything down. By now, you are ready to look at what you've been thinking about and start the journey to making it a reality. The hard work can now begin; you can take what you've written and move towards working on a business plan and outline.

It's important to note that the one difference between conceiving a child and a business is that in business, conception never stops. From brainstorming to writing, it never stops. Every new thought and addition to the journey involves this same process. So now you have conceived, but this is only the beginning; now the work continues full steam ahead.

Chapter 3: **You're Pregnant!!**

Well it's official; you're pregnant! After weeks, months, or years of trying to conceive, you are officially pregnant with the vision for your business and brand. You have great ideas and you've written them down so now is the time to find the people, connections, and entities to get your business started. If you aren't sure where to find the answers, you can always start by Googling. Yes, Google it. Let me just point out that my previous statement is a great example of branding success. Not only have Google's branding methods turned them into a verb; they have also given them the reputation of being a resource for all things.

Ok, I must stop here because unconsciously we have stumbled across a great branding example, so please indulge me. When I suggested that you "Google it," I was merely stating that a great starting point for finding information as it relates to your brand is to do an Internet search. Google is actually a search engine. You can really use any search engine, but because of their awesome branding, we automatically default to Google. Google has been so consistent with their brand's reputation of being an informational source that it is almost the equivalent of having a monopoly over the Internet.

When your brand is so solid and effective, it becomes second nature to your consumers or clients. Without even thinking your clients will automatically default to your brand because if you've given it the time and effort required to establish it, your brand will stand out among the others. Here's another question for you to ponder. What is it going to take for you to have a brand that your audience automatically identifies with? Don't answer that now, just write down the question and really think about the answer as we progress through the book. The great part of this new pregnancy of yours is that you have the time to grow and develop these ideas and figure out thoughtful answers to the questions that I pose.

Ok. Now back to your pregnancy. How are you feeling? Are you experiencing any nausea, anxiety, or nervousness? I'm sure that you are and if so, that's normal because this branding and business venture is a big step that you've taken. Birthing a business is risky, it's tiring, there are no guarantees and it is incredibly time consuming. There are a lot of sleepless nights, aches and pains, and don't get me started on those times when situations become uncomfortable; but with all that comes great reward. The reward of a successful business, satisfied clients, growth and sustainability are so extremely gratifying that everything else is totally worth it.

So prior to my Google revelation, I was mentioning that a great starting point for you is to research other businesses and experts in your field. Research what it takes to become recognized as a legitimate business in your state, then do all of the necessary groundwork to make that happen. Talk to business lawyers and professionals who can guide you through that process and follow the advice that they provide. It is not a hard process at all, but you should seek guidance on that aspect of the business so that you don't have to back track later on. As a PR and branding expert, I am not qualified to advise you on the legal aspects of your business, but I can tell you that now, during the pregnancy, is the time to actually handle that process. Now you can work out all of the kinks, and details associated with starting your business so that after you give birth, you can direct your entire focus on your brand identity and development.

A simple Internet search will point you in the direction of finding legal professionals in your area. If nothing else you will at least find some content that will advise you of the process. From a PR and branding component I am recommending this so that you can read articles and find experts, bloggers, conferences, seminars, and workshops that you can connect with through conversation and networking. You will learn tips from others who have blazed trails on the same journey that you are about to embark. Now listen carefully, I said that Internet research is a starting point, it is not the *only* point. To be successful in any business, you must find a way to interact with the people in your industry. You need to talk to people and connect with people who are successful at what you are trying to do. Read books, talk to experts, and reach out to organizations to see if you can shadow someone who is doing what you want to do. You can even consider going back to school or at least taking a few classes or refresher courses to help you perfect your craft. Be creative in your approach to finding information. The information is out there and you definitely want to be as informed as possible.

When I was pregnant with Aria, I think that I may have read every pregnancy and parenting book and article that was ever written. If not, it sure felt that way. I wanted to be extra prepared; quite frankly, because I didn't want to do anything that would send my child to therapy later in life. I'm saying that jokingly, but I'm also serious. As a first time parent—and I'm sure it doesn't change for parents of multiple children—you can truly stress yourself out by trying to know everything there is to know about your child before he or she even arrives. We place a lot of pressure on ourselves to parent perfectly.

My husband and I attended classes, watched videos, read articles, talked to other parents, talked with our parents, and through that formed our own philosophies and parenting tactics. Now I mentioned this before and it bears repeating; everything that we read and thought that we learned did not work when we tried to apply it to our child, but at least we had a starting point. All those books, classes, and talks, were helpful though, because the knowledge provided us with a good foundation. That is the same process that you are embarking on right now. Everything that you read and learn through your research will not necessarily be the way that you will ultimately operate your business practice, but at least it gives you a foundation. **Learn the rules before you break the rules,** or as Pablo Picasso said, "Learn the rules like a pro, so you can break the rules like an artist."

I think that is an important lesson for an entrepreneur or business leader. A large part of the reason that we chose this profession is because we want to do things our own way. As an entrepreneur, you love the idea of being your own boss and making your own rules. I am a firm advocate of doing so as well, but only *after* you learn the art of your industry. Think of it this way, babies have to learn how to walk before they can run. They start by crawling and learning balance. Then they move on to standing up and taking small steps by holding on to something, such as the couch. Finally, they get the nerve to take a step or two only before falling back down.

This process goes on and on for a while—some longer than others—but after the child learns how to walk, they are able to run, jump, skip, flip, dive, and pretty much everything else in addition to walking. Somewhere along the way, they continue to practice and learn what they were supposed to do before they tried doing things differently. The child didn't start running from birth; he or she had to work hard to get to the point of running. The same is true for you. During this pregnancy phase and beyond, put in the effort to learn your craft. After all, your clients will be able to decipher if you are truly skilled at what you do.

A large part of my research for birthing both my child and my business came from connecting with others who were experienced in what I was trying to learn. Simply put, this is the art of networking. Networking is a term that you will hear all throughout this book. The power of networking can take you further than just about any other business tactic. If you place yourself in close proximity to those who are already successful at what you want to do, then you can monitor them, talk with them and learn from them. If you are a hairstylist and you have aspirations of owning your own salon, then you should reach out to several salon owners who own the type of salon that you wish to open. Learn from them, ask questions, shadow them, and then stay connected to them. This is the case with any brand.

There is a learning opportunity available in every experience and encounter that you have. I feel as though I have learned more about what I *don't* want my brand to be from others than what I *want* my brand to be. If you attend an event and meet people that you would rather not connect with, that is ok. You can still learn from them; you can learn how you *don't* want to operate. Learning comes in all shapes and forms. Don't despise this part of the process and don't ignore the art of networking. All of this helps you learn what elements you will use to lay the foundation for your business and brand; and a solid foundation for your business will yield exponential results later on.

I can honestly say that just about every aspect of my career from the opened doors to the new opportunities, to the clients that I've worked with, can all link back to some form of networking. That's just the world that we live in; who you know definitely carries more weight than what you know. Our world has become so focused on instant gratification that people are always searching for an easier solution. Quite frankly it's just easier, in this fast paced society, to eliminate a lot of searching, filtering, and reviewing by just reaching out to networks for the perfect person or candidate for an opportunity.

I am an only child and I have never had a problem doing things on my own. I love people and interacting with them, but I have never had a problem being alone. When I first started my business, I didn't recognize the value of networking. I really disliked going to conferences or professional meetings because I felt that they were a waste of time and that I could better spend my time doing other things. I soon realized that not even I could embark on this journey by myself. Even if you are in business alone, you still need others constantly throughout the process.

No matter how innovative our world becomes, no one will ever be able to conceive alone. With the latest advances in technology and the miracle of modern breakthrough, the process of fertilization will never change. Even single parents need the assistance of someone else, whether it is family, friends, a baby sitter, a doctor, or a tutor. No matter the need, people need other people. The same goes for your business. You may need social media for your business but you may not be a social media expert. If that's the case then you must connect with someone in some capacity who is a social media expert so that you can either learn social media to handle it yourself or hire someone who will handle it for you. The same goes for any area of business that requires you to gain assistance.

Further along in this book I will go into great detail about networking because it is that important to really dissect ways to capitalize on the power of networking. We all have to realize that we are not the experts in all things related to starting and growing our businesses. Be open and willing to receive help and guidance. Don't pretend to have it all figured out, because going it alone has the potential for disaster. Remember, an effective brand is when your identity matches with your reputation. Faking it until you make it, is not the secret to success, in fact it is the secret to being exposed for being "fake."

Let's discuss for a moment the barriers and pitfalls of this journey. As you wrote down your vision and ideas when you were conceiving earlier, you also wrote down your questions. Now that we are further along in the pregnancy, it's time to look at the things that you've written down, (i.e. your ideas and growth plans) and start formulating a true business model. This will include the barriers that you have now, deciding what the short-, mid-, and long-term goals and action plans are, and looking at realistically prioritizing the steps towards birthing your business.

Now this book does not go in-depth into developing a business plan. What we will discuss for the rest of this chapter is how to develop a strategic plan for your business. You may be thinking, "I thought that we were going to talk more about branding." Well, this is all a part of the branding process, because just like in your personal life, if you don't really know who you are then you can't accurately portray yourself to the public. Once you really have a handle on what you want your business to be, you will have no problem branding it. Everything will align and aspects of the brand identity, such as developing your business cards, logo, website, will basically already be established. The only thing left would be for you to be creative in your design process and that's the easy part!

By the time my husband and I were pregnant, we had already confirmed the name for our child. We did not yet know the gender, but had chosen options for both boy and girl names. This is how we picked it: remember earlier, I talked about how we thought about everything from her personality to her grandkids? We based the names on the type of personality and reputation that we hoped that he or she would have. I'll only talk about my daughter's name since that's who we ended up having.

We knew that we wanted her to feel a sense of self-worth; we wanted her to have pride in herself and carry herself as though she was the most precious person in the world. Not arrogant, but full of self-esteem. Ideally a person like this will also have the same sense of care and compassion for others as well and that's who we wanted her to be. Based on these characteristics, we chose the middle name Jayde (pronounced Jade). We chose to add the "y" in there because we also wanted her to be unique and feel different (in a good way). Studies have proven that self-esteem and self-worth for everyone, but especially a woman, are critically important in the type of person that the person becomes. So we picked her ideal characteristics, and chose her middle name based on those qualities that we hoped she would possess.

We wanted her to feel that she was a rare, and special jewel in hopes that she would believe that and portray herself in a way that aligned with the image that her name represents. When you choose your business name, identify the qualities that will make your brand unique and stand out and align the name—and every other aspect of the business—around that image. It holds you accountable to the brand's reputation. It serves as a reminder of what your brand represents and it also reinforces this image and reputation to your audience.

We also thought of our daughter's potential interests and hobbies and the things that provide us (her parents) joy, peace, and happiness. For me, music has always been such a vital part of my life. I love to sing and play instruments and just listen to all types of music. I chose the first name Aria for her because of my love for music and what it represents. The musical definition for Aria is a "beautiful soprano melody." Arias are known to be soothing, beautiful, and melodious. Music is also an international language. It sees no color, gender, ethnicity, and it provides healing, and unity throughout the entire world. To many others, and me, it represents peace.

I wanted those same types of characteristics, which were indicative of compassion, to be associated with my daughter. So together, her name is Aria Jayde: a beautiful melody and a precious gemstone. Now that she is here, my husband and I have the task of molding her and guiding her to have that identity (or something quite similar) that we envisioned for her. That's the job of a parent. Although, just like your child, your business will grow into its own, you as the overseer are charged with the responsibility of making sure that any changes or evolutions that happen are in line with the identity that you've envisioned for your "baby." So choose wisely concerning everything pertaining to your business. Be very selective and meticulous about everything that has the potential to affect your company's reputation and image.

The process that I used to prepare for the birth of my child, is the same process that I use, and that I coach others to use, to develop their brands. **Let the name, logos, website and all of those smaller aspects of the brand identity come after you have really determined the identity, values, and core foundation of your business.** I should mention this also: Four years later at the time of my writing this book, my daughter is truly living up to her name. There are and always will be obstacles here and there but not only does she love life and music, she loves people and is generally a good and respectable child. She is turning out to be just what we envisioned she would be, which is encouraging but it also further emphasizes our role as parents in keeping her on that path. This same concept applies to your brand. There is value in being thoughtful and intentional in achieving your goals.

So how do we do this? It happens by doing what I mentioned earlier. Taking those ideas and all the aspects that you envisioned and wrote down, and prioritizing them. Think about the answers to questions such as:

- What are realistic steps in this process currently?
- What are my immediate needs?

- What types of resources do I have to get started?
- What are my limitations and how do I work around them?

These and others are questions that need to be answered in order to hit the ground running. Remember this, the answers to these questions will come. You don't have to answer them at once. Some questions you just may not know at this point; and that's ok. Some answers will come after you have visited your mentors and workshops and researched a bit.

This is the pregnancy phase; this is your time of preparation and planning. Use this time to figure out the answers. The wonderful thing is that you are not on anyone's deadline other than your own. Create deadlines, but also be realistic. As you gain a few answers, you will have more questions. Those questions will lead to even more answers and ideas. The key is persistence and hard work. Every successful entrepreneur and businessperson has first and foremost attributed his or her success to hard work. Remember the quote from Vince Lombardi? Nothing worth having comes easily but hard work and determination really do pay off.

Let's pretend that you have all of the answers to the basic questions that you've asked. You know what you want your business to stand for. You know your limitations for your business. You know your strengths and weaknesses; and you've answered other questions that are specific to your areas of expertise.

Remember that these are not the only questions that you will need to ask, I am just providing a few starter questions to get the ideas flowing. You know better than anyone what you don't know.

Again, we are pretending to have all of the answers to the questions that you wrote down. Now based on the answers, prioritize what you can and cannot do realistically right now. Remember this does not mean that you can never do them, it just means that right now at this point in your process you are going to focus on other areas. As you begin to prioritize, the aspects that are within reach—or at least are attainable now—should be short-term goals. **Short term doesn't mean this week! Don't rush the process.** Depending on how far in advance you are planning, short term could mean between right now and two years from now. Within each short-, mid-, and long-term plan, prioritize those items by what can be done sooner and what can be done later.

For example, let's say that you've listed the following short-term goals:

- develop a website
- secure a business location
- finalize my brand
- acquire a business license

These are very generic goals for the sake of the example, but looking at them I would categorize this way:

- Finalize my brand (deadline two months)
- Acquire a business license (deadline three to four months)
- Develop a website (deadline six months to one year)
- Secure a business location (one to two years)

Your plan will look much more organized and detailed than my bullets above, but you get the idea.

I also recommend putting notes by each goal, such as who to contact or the names of people who specialize in the area of the goal you want to reach. Remember to write as much down as possible. Everything jumbled in your head only creates confusion and aggravation. But the sample plan above is an example of how to prioritize your goals. It may take more or less time than you have allotted and that's fine because you can always adjust. The key is to be prepared and be realistic and get started. There is nothing worse than starting your business and then having to close it down after six months to a year because the proper groundwork wasn't established beforehand. You're pregnant! The great thing about this pregnancy is that you determine when you give birth.

55

ς

Chapter 4: **The Shining Star**

This is one of the shortest chapters in this book, but if you are able to figure this one out, you may have found the golden ticket to the road to your success. Before we get into what makes you unique, I would like to point out something. A lot of what I am sharing with you will evolve into a starting point for a marketing plan and a full-fledged public relations strategy. It's important that I say this because at times, the entire process outlined in this book illustrates how important it is to incorporate public relations into the very beginning of the conversation about your business. I've explained before how potential clients will come to me with their completed business plan and want me to add the PR piece afterwards. The result is a complete restructure of so many vital pieces to their plans because they didn't initially consider PR.

Including the PR aspect from the very beginning eliminates contradictions and miscommunication when it comes to branding. You cannot start a business, publicize your business, and then after you gain public interest decide, "oops, I need a website," or "oops, I don't have any long-term goals," or "oops, I didn't consider what I want people to understand about my brand." Well, you can do it that way, but I certainly would not advise that. The best planner still ends up with questions about next steps or restructuring due to an unexpected occurrence, but with the right focus on the marketing, business and PR strategies, you are less likely to find yourselves having to start from scratch or worse, waste money rebranding and strategizing because from the beginning your plan wasn't developed effectively.

I must stress the importance of this part of the process, because the more effort you expend on the front end, the less revamping you will need to do in the future. One thing that I talked about earlier with establishing your brand's identity is thinking about what sets you apart from the competition. That is what we are going to dive into now. Finding your niche, your uniqueness, and your area of strength will make it so much easier to identify your brand and brand identity. I will be totally honest; this is not an easy task. It requires a lot of thought, but when you figure it out, moving forward with your PR strategy is so much easier.

Let me pull out my faux psychology degree for a moment and say this, **a person who does not really understand themselves can't communicate or demonstrate who they are to others.** The same goes for a business, if you haven't really thought about the characteristics of your business, how can you communicate why the public should invest in it? I don't mean an actual investor; I mean your customers or your audience and supporters.

The people who will spend their money to utilize your product or service should feel that it is worth their hard earned money to patronize your business. So why should they? What is it about you (if you are the brand) or your business that is so great that it wins over all of the other businesses out there like yours? As hard as it may be to answer this question, there is an answer and until you have it, you are not ready to push your business to the public. Don't worry; my goal is to help you find the answer! When you are able to pinpoint your business identity, you've actually made tremendous strides toward developing your marketing strategy and PR plan. As I mentioned earlier, I won't get into the marketing strategy piece, but just know that you will have that component of the strategy when you need it.

I would like to recommend that you create a business statement. If you would like to view it as a mission statement, that's fine, but the statement, whether formal or informal, should incorporate characteristics of your brand. It will keep you accountable and it will help you stay on track with the original purpose of the business. Your business statement sums up the "moral of the story" for your business.

Have you ever read a book or a parable and at the end of your reading thought about the moral of the story? Perhaps you have heard the common phrase, "everything happens for a reason." Well that reason, or moral of the story, is the "why" behind why your business exists. Remember back to when you were in the conception phase of the business; you had that vision based on something that you believed in, or your own personal experience or interest. Maybe you are just extremely talented or interested in a particular area and you would love to make that interest or talent a career. Whatever the case may be, there is a reason that you decided to make a business out of whatever it is that you do.

Consider a person who has started a non-profit organization that mentors young, fatherless males. That person may have started the nonprofit due to his or her own childhood experience. This new entrepreneur may have grown up without a father, which had a devastating effect on him. Now the business owner has a non-profit that specifically caters to young, fatherless boys. That's the "why." Why did you start this business? If asked this question, that entrepreneur's answer may be:

> "Because at one point in my life, I was one of those kids that I serve today. I know what they are going through and how they feel. I know that they need a shoulder to cry on and a friend to talk to. I know that they want to feel like someone understands."

Drawing on personal experiences or areas of interest helps to determine the focus of your brand. We are all unique and the great thing about that is no matter how many products, services, or speakers there are in the world that are similar to yours, you have a unique story, experience, or skill that can make you stand out. The key is to define what that is and use it to its fullest capacity to market your business.

In our example above, maybe one of the attributes of the nonprofit's brand could be empathy. Perhaps the uniqueness of this organization is that it only utilizes mentors who also were fatherless boys. General volunteers and staff may be used in other areas, but when it comes specifically to mentoring the boys, they could be paired solely with someone who has traveled the same path. This approach may be a unique aspect of the program that sets them apart. Other nonprofits may utilize anyone who is ready and willing to mentor, but this nonprofit is different in its approach.

After measuring the effectiveness of the mentorship program, results could suggest that this particular nonprofit has a better success rate than others similar. In my mind our fictitious non-profit is not well known for its accomplishments and approach. Some branding characteristics could be community outreach, empathy, and reciprocation. The community outreach aspect is self-explanatory and we've discussed the empathy, but the reciprocation could stem from not only mentoring the young males but training them to in return give back by becoming mentors as well. As the entrepreneur thinks and plans more, so many other ideas will come and they will develop other ways to stand out and be successful but this is the process for figuring out what direction your brand should head.

Now of course this is just an example, but one thing to remember is that if you make a bold claim about your business, or you find your brand's niche, you have to live up to that proclamation. In the case of our nonprofit example that means that if empathy is one of our characteristics and the entrepreneur brands the company around that idea with slogans and messaging, the company can't renege later on. Does that mean that they must forever stick to solely targeting fatherless boys? No. What that does mean is that as they grow and evolve they should find ways to still maintain that brand.

It's imperative that a company find ways to remain relevant but the trick is to figure out how to do that without changing the identity of the company. Even when companies rebrand, they should find ways to do so without becoming a totally different, unrecognizable company. The "fatherless males mentoring" nonprofit may decide to branch out and later on serve fatherless girls, or orphans, or battered women, the possibilities are endless but they can still do all of these things while remaining true to their brand. The mentors for each of the new areas can still be relatable, they can still train the mentees to become future mentors later on, they can still become trusted within the community and partner with other organizations. The growth does not have to stop; it just needs to be consistent with the brand, which is why effectively defining the brand initially is so important.

Do brands change? Short answer: yes. Brands change for a number of reasons, but I've observed that the majority of the time, it is best for the brand to expand rather than change. Expansion equates to growth. Change usually (not always) indicates that there was a problem or issue that needed to be revamped. Brands expand all of the time and in my opinion, that reflects an awareness of the changes in the industry and the leadership, and the ability to reflect that change within the business.

What happens when your unique brand has become obsolete due to changes in that industry? Two things can happen: You can find an innovative way to remain relevant. The great thing about changes in the industry is that they don't happen overnight. It's important to constantly monitor trends in your industry, changes, communicate with your audience to see how they still feel about your product or service. Communicate with others at networking events and conferences to find out what the projected trends will be in the next year or the next five to ten years. Start strategizing ahead of time to find out how you will adjust to your industry's change.

Take the newspaper industry, for example. There was once a time that the newspaper was a preferred source of news information. People picked up their paper off of their front porch or at the newsstand and read it over their morning coffee or after their evening dinner (very Leave it to Beaver, I know but it's true). Over time, other methods of communication started to form and become more popular. Television news, that at one point was only televised once a day, started airing more and more news telecasts. Nowadays it seems that at any given point throughout the day there is a newscast on somewhere on someone's channel. Because it was easier to learn the latest information by just turning on the television, newspapers soon became less popular. Over the past decades, methods for gathering news have become so vast that it would take a separate book to talk about its evolution, but if you notice, newspaper outlets have managed to remain vital to the field.

This is an example of adapting to the trends in your industry. The way we receive news now is nothing like it was decades ago. Where the newspaper once dominated, it now fights to compete with the other myriad of news outlets but it has remained competitive and for some papers, it is a frontrunner. What changed about their brands? For mainstream newspapers such as LA Times, Wall Street Journal, USA Today, Washington Post and others, nothing really changed about the brand but everything changed about the delivery of the brand.

These types of papers now offer up-to-date, online and mobile website access, smartphone access, and social media channels that remain active. Rather than only once or twice a day updates, they compete with their broadcast counterparts with breaking news apps, and some even provide video on their websites. They didn't have to change their brands; they just expanded them. Most importantly, they didn't have to shut down and close their doors, they remain at the forefront of media access by recognizing ahead of time the changing industry and acting accordingly.

On the other hand, if the company's brand is so unique that they can't find a way to expand with the changing trends (although there is always a way), then the inevitable may happen. I'll give you an example. Do you remember Polaroid? Polaroid was the instant picture company that was a hit around the 1960's. People were able to "instantly" develop pictures from their cameras and everyone had a Polaroid. I suppose that we have always been a society that enjoys instant satisfaction. My mother's photo albums from my childhood are filled with Polaroid pictures. At that time the alternative was to pack up the family, venture out to a portrait studio, and wait for a very long period of time to receive the photos. Well that was great for Polaroid because people wanted their pictures a little sooner and Polaroid was *the* go-to brand. They found their uniqueness and capitalized on it.

By the time our society moved on to total electronic photo frenzy, along with the development of the camera phone and shopping centers that carry one-hour photo and instant prints, Polaroid became less of a necessity. By the time we stopped developing pictures altogether and opened photo storage and sharing accounts, Polaroid cameras were obsolete. I dare not forget to mention that at one point cameras were getting smaller and smaller with electronic photo sharing capabilities also.

The company did not find a strong way to stay relevant and innovative with the cameras during the transition to electronic photos and ultimately halted production of its cameras in the early 2000s. Had Polaroid recognized the pending cultural change ahead of time they may have been able to identify ways to stay relevant in the photography industry. Some sources have divulged that the company was not optimistic that there would ever be a time that people did not prefer a paper photo.

The moral of this story is that being unique and standing out is a great thing always, but with a brand you have to remain aware and you must never stop thinking and strategizing for ways to keep the brand alive. I never recommend holding back on the creativity, even it if is not appropriate for "now;" store that idea because you never know how quickly the appropriate time will come. So let's end this chapter by starting the brainstorming process of figuring out how to make your brand stand out.

To do this you will need to do a little research. Ask yourself our core questions, such as:

- Why do I want this business? This answer can range from anything such as to change a public policy, to create a safe and reliable product, to make more money (I hope that's not the only answer), to help young children, to just about anything under the sun. There is no wrong answer, just write them all down and prioritize them.

- Who needs my business and why? We will ask this question again for a more in depth answer when we start thinking about our target audience, but it is always appropriate to start thinking about who you want to reach and why you want to reach them. Hint: Everyone is not a good answer! Let's try to narrow that down a bit and if it still expands to everyone, then great, but we definitely need a starting point.

- What is the moral of my story? This means that at the end of the day the people you reach will look, feel, believe, or experience what? This is an important question because the answer to this question is what you plan to deliver to your clients. Really think about this answer because once you brand it this way, people will expect you to keep your word.

- What is the most out-of-the-box method for my product or service to perform? I like this question because the sky is the limit. Everything that you write down has the potential to work. All of your answers (because you are required to have more than one answer for all of these) may not be appropriate right now, but there could definitely be a place or variation of these ideas at some point throughout this journey.

Remember that in all of your planning you are not just thinking for the start of your business. You are thinking in terms of longevity. After you have some of the answers, start prioritizing and connecting them and before you know it you will have the characteristics of your brand that actually make sense to you.

Chapter 5: Brand Spanking You!

I would like to start this chapter by saying that everything that you will read in this book applies also to your personal brand. The concepts of branding are really no different for those with a business brand than they are for those with a personal brand. I felt however that it was important to take a moment to talk specifically about the personal brand to highlight the similarities when you are intentionally the brand and to point out that whether intentional or not, *you* are still a brand.

Every branding book and expert that you encounter will tell you to keep your personal and professional life separate. This is true in theory, this is true in corporate America, and this is true in most cases from the aspect of legal protection all the way to your social media pages. As with just about everything else that we have discussed, there is always an exception to the rule. In this case the exception has two parts, the first is when *you* are the brand and the other is when you are *not* the brand! Confusing? Great! That means that I have your attention. The bottom line is that there is a very blurred line between you and your business on all accounts, especially when it comes to branding.

Whether you're intentional or not, you are a brand. We've already learned that a brand is an identity or reputation right? Well, you—the person—have an identity that in turn becomes you—the brand. Just go ahead and accept it, you are a brand. Your family is part of your brand, your career is part of your brand and yes, what you do personally, also affects your brand.

If you start embracing the idea of you as the brand, you will proceed accordingly. Let's talk about this. Let's go back to our core questions. How do you want people to view you? How should people identify you? What is your reputation? For those of you who are not motivational speakers, authors, musicians, or any other type of business where your name is your business, these next few pages are for you. Don't worry though, for those of you who are the aforementioned business or other types of personal brands that I did not mention, this still applies but I have more for you coming right up.

With personal brands it is so important that you portray yourself in a way that you can actually keep up with. The best way to do that is to be "real" (as the young people say). That simply means to be you. In an earlier chapter we talked about identifying the characteristics of your business such as what makes it stand out, why do people need it, and what are the most creative ways to reach your target audience. These questions apply to the personal brand as well. If you build your personal brand based on your own key attributes, then it is so much easier to become trustworthy to your audience. There is no worst "brand killer" than for an audience to find out that the brand was a fake.

Let me stay right here for a moment and talk more about a trustworthy personal brand. Our society makes it very difficult to hide who we really are. With so many variations of social media, along with instant messaging, live video streams, reality TV, and streaming websites, maintaining a façade would be really hard work. Take for example a person who may be a fitness and nutrition guru known for his or her fabulous body, healthy eating, and very strict diet. Let's imagine that this person has thousands of followers on their various social media channels. They have profited millions with speaking engagements, fad diets, exercise videos, and various workouts and exercise techniques. Our fictitious fitness guru has created the perfect personal brand that people love and trust.

Let's imagine now that after the numerous appearances on talk shows, and the combined millions of dollars that the target audience has spent on products and services, this person was recorded saying that they really achieve their physique due to steroid use or that they are able to maintain the body that everyone aspires to have with plastic surgery. Not only would this information be devastating and discouraging to the person's target audience, their personal brand has officially taken a turn for the worse.

People prefer honesty and transparency from their businesses. They want the truth about the product, the anticipated results and the people in charge of the product. I can't begin to name how many companies have plummeted thanks to unethical leadership or a loss of trust by the clients. **Even if the intention of a company's brand is sincere, a contradiction of the brand is business suicide. Especially when the target audience finds out about the contradiction in any way other than the horse's mouth.**

Let me repeat that.   A contradiction of the brand is business suicide. In other words, don't pretend to be who you are not; especially with your personal brand.   There are too many avenues available for people to watch your every move 24/7 and keeping up a façade is too challenging and unrealistic to be successful.

Realizing now that you are a brand whether you like it or not, try to identify ways to incorporate your beliefs, values, interests, and talents into your brand.   Your business started because you enjoy doing something or you really believe in a cause or mission, so now continue to incorporate you into the brand and brand identity. This includes anything from adding your favorite color as part of the logo to using your name or ancestor's name as part of your business name.

Chick-fil-A restaurants took on the characteristics of the founders, rather than the founders tailoring themselves to their idea of what the restaurant should be. They believe in family and togetherness and as a result the stores are not open on Sundays because they believe that families should be together on Sunday. They have a passion for youth so the restaurants hire a very large number of youth and provide scholastic incentives for their employees. This aspect and others have led to the success of this restaurant and the longstanding respect for the family.

As a personal brand, what are you promising your customer? Are you really able to deliver that promise? How do you view yourself? How does your audience view you? These are just a few of the questions that you should ask yourself when determining your personal brand. I have a question for you and I want you to think carefully about this answer. Do you have a way to gauge your personal brand's reputation with your clients? This is an important question because you definitely need to know what your customers are saying about you. Do they believe in what you are selling to them? Why or why not? Once you find the answers to these questions, then you can adjust accordingly to make sure that at the end of the business day you are holding true to your brand.

What does your personal brand look like? May I discuss social media for a moment? Thanks. Social media can be your best friend or worst enemy. Nothing is a secret on social media so it is so important to be strategic even with what you are posting about your brand. Let's start with your followers. For your business page, your followers should be an indicator of your brand. If I were to look solely at your followers before I even looked once at your actual social media page content, your followers should be a reflection of your brand. This is regarding social media for your business. If you are a fitness guru, I should be able to tell that by looking at your followers. Don't get me wrong, I do recognize that with a public social media account, you cannot control who follows you, but **if your content reflects your brand, then the majority of your followers will also.**

A fitness expert's social media followers should consist of workout enthusiasts, other fitness experts, gyms, fitness equipment brands, and anything or anyone else that falls under the fitness category. How does this happen, you ask? What you are posting and hashtagging will show up on the pages of others who are interested in the same things that you are. A hairstylist should post before and after photos of her work, and perhaps client testimonials or photos of other stylists' work. As a result, their followers should consist of all things hair and beauty. Looking at your followers will help determine whether or not your page is truly reflective of your brand.

The other piece of the social media conversation is that you should actually be active on social media. Don't just have an account and never or rarely use it. I don't mean that you have to post something five times a day every day because then I have to question if you are actually getting work done. But you should be communicating with your followers and "meeting potential followers" on social media and by doing so, you are also finding out their interests, dislikes, trends etc. Social media is a tool that will definitely help boost personal and business brands, but as with everything else that we have discussed so far in this book, it does require strategy.

Social media right now is your own private community of clients. They can find out more about you and whether your brand is trustworthy and you can find out more about them and ways to keep them engaged based on the feedback that you are receiving. I have a client that is so knowledgeable of her audience that she knows the best time to post on her social media accounts based on her audience. She doesn't post during their peak work hours because more than likely her followers are not on social media. She posts in the morning before work hours and late evening around rush hour when people are finally off from work. She based this off of what days and times she received the most "likes" on social media. She did the research, communicated with her followers, stayed true to her brand and now when she posts a photo or comment, her audience immediately communicates back with her.

Since I am a writer, I must warn you that this next topic is a huge pet peeve of mine. When posting to your social media website or even sending written communication, it is so important to make sure that your communication is error free. There is nothing worse than reading material from a business and spotting misspelled words and grammar issues. I am not saying that you have to hire an editor for every single piece of material that you write, but I am saying that you should spellcheck and proofread. Even with social media posts.

I get it. You are posting using your phone; your fingers are a little larger than the letters and numbers on the phone and that darn auto correct keeps changing your words to something else without your written or verbal consent. I get that. I really do; and there is slight forgiveness for misspellings and typos. What I cannot tolerate; however, is the repeated use of misspelled words and a clear indication that the post or written communication piece was not proofread before it was posted.

Yes, I know what you are saying. "Melva, you're a writer; of course you are critical of written communication." Well, yes. You're right, I am a writer; but I'm also someone's customer and these types of posts indicate to me—the customer—that you are not thorough, you don't have much pride in your business, and you may not have the necessary capabilities for handling my business needs. Yes, I get all of that from a poorly or unedited post!

The motto of my company is that writing is the first impression. If writing is the first impression— and is sometimes the only impression—then the writing (even on social media) must be impeccable. Not impeccable in the sense that you need to hire the services of an author or wordsmith, but impeccable in that it is rare that we will find errors. Simple editing, and proofreading before you press post or send is half the battle. I am only trying to say that you should make sure that the message is clear and error free. Don't rush, don't make the post or communication too wordy, and most importantly, make the content in it relevant.

Content is another element that we should discuss. Whether it's content on your website, in your brochure, or your social media accounts, the subject matter should be concise and relevant to your brand. As a personal brand, people are getting to know *you*. They are learning what you know. If you are a person known for having profound posts or sayings, then make sure that they are relevant to your platform. A counselor who specifically targets married couples, for example, would not have the same audience or followers as the fitness expert from earlier. Now, let me say this. There may be some general overlap, but primarily, they will have two different types of followings because of the content that they are distributing.

The marriage counselor may post wedding photos, or memes about vows, and they will probably post testimonials of happy clients. They may post their insight on the latest Hollywood marriage or breakup. Whatever the content may be, it should be relevant to the brand. As cute and adorable as your children are and as fun as your family may be, your personal branding platform—which again, is the platform that promotes you as a brand—should not be inundated with photos of your family vacations, family reunion pictures, and child's dance recital. It's ok to have more than one social media account and the family aspect would be best suited for the family-oriented account. The account that promotes you as a business should cater more toward information that establishes you as the business expert for your brand. Remember, even your personal brand is your business.

There are certain liberties that you can take with personal branding; however, your clients do want to know a bit more about you than if you were, say... the CEO of a large corporate brand. So every now and then I believe that it is fine to allow a peek into your personal life. As I mentioned earlier, the lines are blurred when it comes to personal branding and business branding, but the best way to tell if your personal branding efforts are effective is by looking at who is following you.

I have placed a larger focus on social media in this section because there is such a large opportunity to grow the personal brand through this outlet. It is not the only opportunity by any means, but it is definitely a platform that can do a tremendous amount of damage to a personal brand if the user is not cautious. I am sure that anyone reading this book can recall celebrities, government officials, or friends for that matter, who has gotten themselves into some hot water due to a social media post that were a little too wild. Going back to your values, beliefs, and interests, think carefully about what you post on social media before you have to retract it and make the contrite apology. The contrite apology is the apology that happens about a day after some well-known person has offended the world by posting something that didn't go over well with the general population.

I wouldn't even know where to start with the examples but I am confident that you can think of your favorite celebrity who posted a comment on social media that offended the world, then later (usually the next day) had to retract that statement and apologize. This happens so commonly now that I believe that we, the general public, have become desensitized to the process. Risqué photos, offensive beliefs, and controversial ideals that contradict your brand are key ways to "go viral" and lose the respect of your audience.

This is a big problem with the issue of personal and business branding. If the CEO of a major corporation posts a comment on his or her personal social media account and that comment contradicts what his or her business stands for, that's considered a contradiction and ends up with a loss of trust for the CEO and the company. When determining if you should post a particular comment or photo, ask yourself, "Is this post really worth the potential fallout from my statement?" If the answer is yes, then go for it. If it's no, just stay away from social media for a moment and confide it to your trusted source.

You may be asking me right now, "How can you advise me to choose to ignore something that I really believe in?" Remember this, I never said to ignore what you believe in, I think that there is a great need and responsibility for a leader to state his beliefs to the masses especially when it will bring about a positive change. My concern is when the personal brand and the business brand don't match. It is difficult to be "pro" one thing personally and "anti" the same thing business wise. If this is your dilemma, then you have to make a choice to either let go of the public proclamation of your personal belief or reevaluate your business brand, because once the contradiction becomes public knowledge, it will place your company in a very awkward and uncomfortable position.

If you find yourself in a situation where your personal beliefs are not lining up with your business' brand, it may be time to reevaluate the business model and ask yourself again the questions that you initially answered in the conception phase. The main objective is for you to be able to live up to your brand.

Chapter 6: Congrats... it's a brand!

Well, it's that time! After months, or in some cases, even years of planning, preparing, researching, writing, and learning, it is now time to birth this brand. In these last few moments of delivery, let's review the checklist to make sure that it is indeed time to PUSH this brand out.

First, do you have general answers to these questions?

1. What exactly is it that I do?
2. What is my brand?
3. How can I make my brand last?
4. Can I live up to my brand's reputation? How?
5. Do I have a vision for how my brand can grow?
6. Who are my customers/clients?
7. What are the real needs of my customers/clients?
8. What am I promising to my customers/clients?

9. How can I present my product or service differently than the competitors?

10. Are my ideas and goals written down and prioritized?

You do not need perfect answers to these questions and they are certainly not etched in stone. They are however important branding questions that you should have at least considered before making further strides toward your business. I must also point out that this book is strictly about the branding and public relations aspects of starting a business. It does not include any of the legal components to starting a business. During your "pregnancy" you should also receive guidance on the necessary steps to have your brand legally protected and recognized as a business in your state.

Are your personal property and finances protected legally in the case of a business pitfall? Do you know the difference between a corporation, LLC, sole proprietorship, and partnership? If you and a partner are going into business, have you sought legal counsel to make sure that everything is written and agreed upon before moving forward? My hope is that by the time you "deliver" you also have both the legal requirements for starting a business and the branding foundation in order. If the legal questions that I just asked are completely foreign to you, then stop! Delivery was a false alarm and there is a little more pregnancy left. Go back and get those legal components in order. I am not a lawyer, but I can tell you that you do not want to move forward with your business until those questions and others have been settled.

Having said that, let's now assume that you have everything in place legally and are now at a good starting point as far as branding is concerned. Since that is the case, then let me be the first to say: Congratulations! It's a Brand!!

You are now the proud parent of a healthy new brand! This point is the beginning of an exciting yet terrifying and highly rewarding, yet frustrating journey of your career. It will be filled with great anticipation and also great hesitation at times. I know that those last statements made absolutely no sense, but I can tell you that as the mother of both a daughter and a business, my previous statement is probably the most accurate statement you will hear on this journey.

So now what? Let's get into the "what's next" phase.   I remember when I gave birth to Aria, it was as if all of those adjectives that I just described to you consumed me all at once. I was so excited to meet her, yet terrified that the doctors and hospital administration were going to send her home with my husband and me. What were they thinking!!   Since she was our first child, we had no idea what was really in store, but we knew that we wanted to do every single thing concerning her the right way. We wanted her to be smart, polite, friendly, athletic, ethical, and successful among so many other things. Remember, I told you earlier that we had her entire life pretty much mapped out, according to our vision, before she was even conceived. When the reality set in that we were solely responsible for guiding her to achieve all of those goals, I think that we both felt totally unequipped. Even after reading so many books and articles from experts on parenting and child rearing a lot of insecurities set it. This happened even though we finally had the child that we prayed for, talked about constantly and watched grow from a little bubble to a full-fledged baby on an ultrasound. She was finally birthed and was placed in our hands, and at that moment the journey began.

Later, on the day she was born, after all of the doctors left the room and the nurses had her nicely swaddled and quiet, I experienced a moment where she and I were the only ones in the room. My husband and family were somewhere else at the time and it was just the two of us. It was really quiet in that room. As I lay there in the hospital bed, I looked over at her and to my surprise it seemed as though she was actually looking back at me. We were staring at each other eye to eye and it was as if we both were saying to the other, "Now what?"

Everything from conception to delivery had happened for this moment and all that was left was to answer the question, "Now what?"

My reason for sharing this is that the exact same thing happens when you birth your business. When you started this experience, your brand was a vision. It was a collection of thoughts and ideas that for whatever reason sparked an interest to pursue it further. It was the moral of a story that in your mind had no limits, no obstacles, and no barriers. The visions turned into more ideas, you planned and researched, attended seminars, spoke to experts, explored all options that were available to you; and now, you've given birth. You have a business model and a plan and everything that happens with this business all leads back to you! After all, the desire to do things your way is part of the reason why you became an entrepreneur, or why you accepted the job as leader of your company, or decided to create a personal brand, right?

You have your name, you know your brand, you followed the legal process and met all of the requirements to become a business and now, with no distractions and no one else in the room, you are looking at your confirmation papers and various registrations and maybe even your business plan... all the components of your brand. It seems as though it's looking back at you and you are both saying, "Now what?"

Now you need clients; now you need growth; you may need a manager or a publicist; you may need an accountant; you may need products; you many need a facility to house your business; you may just need business cards; but at this point, if you are like I was, you are thinking, now the hard part begins. Exciting, right? It actually is. Just like parenting, owning a business is a whirlwind. But to answer your question, my question, and Aria's question, now the work begins!

Just as I learned with my daughter, although I cannot predict the future or know what obstacles and barriers are ahead, I can continue to take the same steps post-partum that I took during conception and pregnancy. What do I mean? With my child and my business, I have never stopped learning, I never stopped visioning, researching, planning, readjusting. I make mistakes and I accomplish goals. Sometimes the actions move according to my plans and other times they take on a life of their own and I adjust but nonetheless, I just take every moment one day at a time. **Each goal that is achieved is just a catapult to the next goal; every lesson learned is merely the foundation to learn more. Every contact gained is an opening to a new relationship and possible venture.** So go ahead and pick up your baby, look at it in awe and take pride in everything that you've accomplished to get to this step. Now that part of the celebration is over so buckle up and let's get to work on this brand!!

Chapter 7: **Seven Qualities of a Successful Brand**

I f you are reading this book, your main question to me is probably, "Melva, how can I gain the attention of the people who need me?" At the end of the day, that is the goal of everyone trying to figure out the best branding tactic for their business. No matter if you are an experienced entrepreneur or just received your business license yesterday, the goal is the same. You want people to know that your brand exists; you want them to remember that your brand exists, and you want them to recognize your brand when they see it. You want to be the go-to resource for your target client.

I think that the key word in that last sentence is "go-to." Let's face it, although your brand is needed, there is a lot of competition out there. There are so many other people who, in some capacity, do what you do. I am not under any delusion that I am the only person out here who is an expert in public relations. I am however confident enough to believe that I am the only person out here who can do public relations the way that I do it. That's the key. You are the best at what you do and there is an audience out there who specifically wants *your* brand. I'll talk about this in a later chapter, but the only true competition out there for you, is you.

When I was preparing to enter high school, I auditioned for their marching band color guard (flag team) during my 8th grade year. During that time high school began at 9th grade and as an 8th grader, I was allowed to audition for the following year's team. The high school was exactly a block away from the middle school that I attended so after school on the first day of try outs, I walked with confidence that one block and entered those high school doors ready to try out. My confidence was quickly broken when I saw the number of older upperclassmen who were also auditioning. They were taller, better, confident, and had way more experience twirling a flag than I did.

When the music started and the color guard captain began to demonstrate the tryout routine, I wanted to turn around and politely slide out the side gym door. It seemed as if she were speaking a different language, moving way too fast for me to keep up, and contorting in ways that I didn't even know were possible for the human body. We didn't have cell phones then, so I couldn't record the routine and watch it at home. I had to try to remember it. Not an easy feat to say the least. Well, I didn't slip out the side door; I stuck around and I did the best that I could for the rest of the rehearsal. When I got home, not only was my body sore but my ego was bruised.

I was a long-time gymnast, a dancer, and pretty athletic so I went into that first day tryout thinking that I would have no problems learning and mastering the routine. So imagine my deep state of depression when I realized that the others, who were older, more experienced and quite frankly, better than me seemed to have no problems keep up and even looked really good just from the first day of tryouts. Well my mother, a very intuitive woman, noticed my lack of enthusiasm about the tryouts and after we talked and I explained everything that I just told you, she looked at me and said, "Melva, there will always be people out here who can do what you do. You can't worry about them; all you can do is what you can do." She made me practice the little bit of routine that I remembered for the rest of the night over and over until I realized that it wasn't really that hard; it was just a matter of learning it my own way. When I went back to the second day of tryouts, I had my confidence back and I was able to perfect the part of the routine that I had practiced the night before and catch on to the next part. I'll fast forward to the end of this story and tell you that because of my determination to be the best that I could be and stand out among all of the others who were doing the exact same routine that I was doing, I was the only freshman on the color guard that year.

Did I want to just share that story with you just to share it? Well actually, yes I did because I like that story, but it is relevant because that is why branding exists. It's a method to help you stand out and be remembered among all of the others who seemingly do the same thing as you. Imagine all of the different brands that exist. There are a lot, I know. Some immediately come to your mind just by thinking of brands, while others may exist that you aren't even aware of. Let's play a quick round of my favorite gameshow, The Family Feud. You are a contestant and I am the host. You say out loud what immediately comes to your mind after I ask this question. Ok, here we go:

We asked 100 people, name a popular shoe brand!

I can hear you now hitting the buzzer and saying, Nike! Ding. Ding. Ding. Ding. Ding.   That's the number one answer! Congratulations. Well depending on your taste, other shoe brands may have also come to mind. If you are interested in an athletic shoe, you may have thought of Nike or Adidas, or another name brand.   If you are interested in a women's designer shoe, you may have named Prada or Christian Louboutin. You thought of the shoe brand that coincided with your particular interest. In my example, I named four different brands between two different categories. There are others that came to mind but then there were hundreds maybe thousands more that I never even thought about. Besides money, why did you and I think of the brands that we thought about? It was solely due to those brands' ability to make an impression based on our interests.

What do I mean?   Prada and Nike are in no way in competition with each other unless one day they decide to cross over into the other's territory. Until then they are like two parallel lines, never to meet. Rather than just branding themselves as "shoes," they capitalized on their specific audience and found ways to brand themselves in a way that is recognizable and effective to their audience.

When a person thinks of Nike he or she will most likely think of a high performance and durable athletic shoe for the most competitive athlete. Commercials, marketing and advertisements and celebrity endorsements all support the idea that this shoe is not only for an athlete, but it's designed for the athlete who wants to win. On the other hand, Prada is a high end, luxury brand. When a person thinks of this shoe, he or she immediately associates it with a hefty price tag, and a classic, luxurious look. Both brands have additional product lines besides shoes that also meet the needs of their clients, but even those lines are relatable to the brand's specific audience.

Just as the two example brands cater to their specific audiences there are other brands, both luxury and athletic, that also have specific audiences. Whereas Nike's shoes are also very attractive and fashionable, another brand may have a more technical shoe with the focus being less on the look of the shoe and more on the operation of the shoe. There may be another athletic shoe brand whose emphasis is less about the performance and more about the appearance or better yet, the price. My point is that these and other brands have mastered the idea of standing out. They have figured out what it takes to reach their audience and they have become successful at it.

So again, there will be an audience for your brand, you just have to tap into it and once you tap into it, you have to find a creative way to stand out among the others. The best way for you to become the number one answer that one hundred people thought of when surveyed on Family Feud, is to figure out what will make your brand successful.

Have no fear; I am here... to help you figure that out. I am going to take you through the seven characteristics (in no particular order) those successful brands possess.

Step 1. Self-Awareness. If you don't understand your brand, no one will. The problem is that because this is your baby, you have tons of ideas in your head ranging from what your brand was, what it is currently, and what it will be in the future. All of those different perspectives can become very cloudy, making it extremely difficult to pinpoint the strengths and realistic characteristics of your brand. On the other hand, you may not have one clue about how any of those attributes relate to your brand. To help figure this out, let's do an organized assessment of the brand by taking a page from the marketing strategist's book and do a SWOT analysis.

A SWOT analysis is an assessment of your company's **(S)**trengths, **(W)**eaknesses, **(O)**pportunities, and potential **(T)**hreats. Understanding the results of your SWOT analysis will help you figure out who you are, why you are that way, and how to capitalize on your characteristics while preparing for future hiccups. The best brands out there have figured out how to implement and capitalize on the analyses to craft a strong business plan and successful brand.

Now it is your turn. Although you can conduct the SWOT analysis alone—and I do recommend that you do some self-reflection on this—it would be great to get a small group of trusted individuals to also conduct a SWOT analysis so that you can compare notes. The group should consist of people who are either part of your team or familiar with your vision for the company. This idea works really well whether you are an established or brand new business.

Strengths – you will notice that everything in this book that I suggest to you will revolve around you answering questions. That's intentional. My job here is not to give you the answers, but to help you start thinking strategically and deeply about your business. I want you to consider aspects of the brand that you may not have known existed. In the excitement of a new business, sometimes the entrepreneur gets stuck on one step: performing the service and reaping the desired results, but there is so much more before, during, and after that process. I really believe in the SWOT analysis because it digs deeply into the areas that are imperative to understand when owning a business. After you view the results of the analysis, the personality of your business should be so much clearer and you can better strategize about your business plan and brand. Trust me, this information will be extremely beneficial as you move forward and experience additional growth.

When thinking of the strengths of the company, answer the following questions with the first being quite simple:

1. **What are your strengths?** This is a self-explanatory question. Really think about the strongest aspects of your business. Although it is a simple question, there is not a simple answer. Strengths do not consist of just, "I can dance," or "I'm a really good writer." Yes, these are strengths, but they are a bit obvious. Of course you can dance; you own a dance studio and of course you are a good writer; you are an author. Let's dig a little deeper.

   So you think you can dance? What is your strongest dance style? Maybe you are a trained ballerina who has traveled the world performing in some of the most well known productions. If this is the case then you may have gained considerable knowledge of the process to become an international ballerina. One of your strengths may be that you have the skillset to train emerging ballerinas in the area of international dance. The list could really go on and on about your strengths, but a great tip that I once received was when you think you've answered the question, dissect that answer even more. Narrow your answers down as far as you can to see all of the options that are available to you. You can select the best ones, after you've completed the process.

2. **What can you offer that is different from the competition?** If there are five people named Jane in a classroom, there will be something different in their personalities alone that will distinguish them from the other four. The same goes for you. There may be five other brands out there that offer the same service as you, but what makes you different?

I have a client who periodically hosts sports training camps. I don't know about you but I always see flyers, especially around the fall and summer, of people hosting boot camps, fitness clinics, and specifically, sports camps. My client had the same vision, but he found his niche.

Not only did he narrow the sport to track and field with an emphasis on hurdlers, but since he is also an Olympic and World Medalist in track and field, his strength is that he is qualified to train others on how to get to his level. Based on that alone, his camp is already set apart from others. Another of his strengths is his network. He expanded his clinic to other areas and invited other Olympians to partner as clinicians, now he has hosted a full sports clinic, titled it the Future Olympians Sports Clinic and I don't think that I have to tell you that he has a tremendous turnout.

His strengths are his skill, his contacts, his experience, and his access to additional resources; which brings me to the next question.

3. **What resources do you possess?** Do you have access to any resources that will help you do your job better? Resources can be people, tangible items, particular software, or whatever will help you overcome any potential obstacles or barriers. Resources can be capital, staff or if you are a seamstress, it could be a sewing machine passed down to you from your grandmother or at least access to a sewing machine. Really think about what you need to build your brand and what you have in place already that will help you in the building process.

I handled PR for a client's event a few years ago and met a really nice caterer. When I attend any event, I always visit with the vendors and get their contact information in case I may need them for my own event or a referral later. At this event I was really impressed with the food so I found the caterer and started a conversation. After talking for a while and complimenting her work, she confided in me that this particular event was only her third event since starting her business. She told me that she worked full time at a facility that had a commercial kitchen that allowed her to use it on the weekends at no cost. In addition, the waiters who were passing around the hors d'oeuvres were her two sons and a nephew.

Talk about resources! Other than food and a few supplies, she practically had every major resource that she needed to get started with her business. I'm sure her sons, nephew and the commercial kitchen were listed on her SWOT analysis as strengths. What are yours?

4. **How does your end result happen?** The first part of this question is "What is your end result?" and the answer to that question was probably answered during the pregnancy phase, but this time when you answer it you can be more concise. No matter what your

business consists of, there is some type of end result to whatever it is that you do. This question is designed to help you analyze that end result. It's basically asking why you are necessary. Not just how you are different but why do people even care about your service or product.

Your original answer to this question will probably be very basic, but the more you think about your answer, the more you are able to focus on key aspects of what you do that will make your brand strong. Your end result may happen quickly or safely, maybe in a calm environment or unique setting. If you are Nike your end result happens triumphantly since the brand focuses on high performance, winning athletes. A speaker's end result may happen clearly, with new insight and motivation. A luxury designer's end result may happen with style or class. Do you see where I am going with this? The answer to this question should be more descriptive. These answers will be the positive factors of the brand and highlight what is readily available to you.

Weaknesses - The competitive disadvantage is what you should think of when you think of the weaknesses of your business. Some of these questions will include:

1. **What is lacking in the business and why?** This question explores the limits and barriers that you are experiencing in your business. To help you put this into perspective think of it this way, if it were not for these aspects, your business would be ahead of the competition or at least further along than it is now.

   For some people money is a weakness. Although I always say that you should never let money stop you from pursuing your dreams, sometimes it does at least slow you down. Staff may be a weakness, maybe you don't have a staff or perhaps your staff may not be the most skilled or the most committed. A weakness could be education. Your competitors may have advanced degrees in the field or a certain type of certification while you may have no formal education at all. Whatever the case is, my advice to you is to find ways to build your weaknesses. Build them so that you can grow and stay comparable to others in your field.

2. **What do I need to improve upon?** This is an honest question because even if things are going fairly well in your business, there is always room for growth. Weaknesses, like strengths, are an internal factor meaning they are things happening from within the company. Improvements will only help you to grow.

3. **What advantages do my competitors have over me?** This a two-sided question because although I am telling you not to compare your business to everyone else's, it is important to be aware of what your competitors are doing and how they are doing it. This information is not to be used to mimic the competition's

brand because you want to stay unique. Instead it is to make sure that your service is on the cutting edge of what is happening in the field and that you are offering the same or higher caliber of product or service than your competition offers.

Opportunities - Opportunities are the external, potentially beneficial situations that are presented or created at any given time. They are sometimes subtle and sometimes not, but the key is to be aware and ready to seize the moments when they arise.

Opportunity questions include:

1. **Can this opportunity strengthen the company's weaknesses?** You listed your company's weaknesses and limitations for a reason. Once you are aware of those weaknesses you become better able to identify opportunities that will eliminate them. Opportunities can come in the form of people, partnerships, trends, or just about anything

else that will help your company become strong in the weak areas and stronger in the strong areas.

2. **Are there any new technologies or trends to take advantage of in your field?** You must be aware of advances in your field. For public speakers, make sure that you know about different social media channels. At one point all we knew of was YouTube, then we learned about Myspace and Facebook and now Instagram, Snapchat and Periscope have taken center stage. I see a lot of public speakers using these platforms for broadcast videos, social media "chats" and other means to stay connected. All of these mediums can help you, the entrepreneur, to connect with your audience and you definitely don't want to be left out of the conversation.

3. **Does my competition have any vulnerability that I can take advantage of?** You are not trying to kick a company while it's down so to speak, with the answer to this

question, but you are trying to find your current or potential competitive advantage.

Let's take a look at Walmart, for example. The company's brand is that prices are cheap. You can visit any Walmart store and find prices lower than basically any of its competitors. In fact, the company slogan is "Everyday Low Prices." Two of the many competitive advantages that Walmart has over the competition is that:

1. The store is able to meet the demands of their customers by innovatively and systematically tracking inventory in a way that other stores have not quite mastered.
2. Walmart has unprecedented negotiating power with its suppliers. A major strength for the store is clearly its ability to force suppliers to lower their prices.

4. **What is my field missing?** This is a great question because if you can find the answer to this question then you have just unveiled the mystery to what will set you apart from the

competitors.   Think   about   the   latest
technologies, things we use now that we
probably never would have imagined being
available to us ten years ago. Those "things"
were someone's idea and as a result, life as we
know it will never be the same.

Threats – The unfortunate thing about threats to
your business is they can come from out of
nowhere. So many unseen sources can become
potential threats. Threats can have both internal
and external implications and must be taken
seriously in order to avoid negative effects on
your company. Here are a few things to consider
about threats:

1. **Are there any potential changes that could
    negatively affect the business?** We know
    that change is hard; and sometimes companies
    do not survive because of change.   This
    question should cause you to look at any threat
    that could consume your business and make
    you to develop an action plan for defeating the
    threat. Is there a change in the economy?   Is

there a shift in trends? Think about the possible answers to these questions as well as potential solutions.

2. **Are you making money or will there be major obstacles to generating income?** This question is important because lack of funding could mean a delayed start or the close of your business. If you haven't started the business yet, think about factors that could hinder you from starting and in both cases implement a plan that will create solutions to these threats. Notice that I didn't say that you will have all of the answers right away, but thinking about these and other potential threats along the way will create less of a shock when they happen. Preparation is key and will help you combat future risks.

3. **What obstacles do your weaknesses present?** This question is important because the weaknesses are issues that are currently present. You've listed the weaknesses already, but now take a look at what current or

potential obstacles can arise because of these weaknesses. Weaknesses are internal factors that are present within your business, so now it's time to think about the potential fallout from these weaknesses.

For instance, if your company will generate income based on the number of employees that you will have, and one of the weaknesses you've listed is that you have a limited number of employees then the potential threat is that you may not be able to meet production demands due to a lack of workers. Whatever you have listed as your weakness, go back and think about how those weaknesses could affect your productivity.

Now that you have completed your SWOT analysis you must look at each category and prioritize them according to what is the most critical. In each area consider what has the greatest potential outcome for each of the most critical aspects of the categories as it relates to your organization. Think about the following questions:

1. How will my strengths complement my opportunities and compensate for my weaknesses and potential threats?

2. What is the best way to supplement and reduce the weaknesses?

3. Which of my strengths really identify the personality of the company.

4. Which of the strengths describe the future of the company.

5. Which opportunities can I capitalize upon that will have the most lasting effects.

The answers to questions three, four, and five, will help you nail down the identity or brand of your business. These answers should mimic how you want to be recognized. The entire SWOT analysis will help you to acquire a better understanding of your brand, how it will operate and the direction that it will take in the future. I should also mention that there is never a bad time to conduct a SWOT analysis. A yearly analysis will help you stay on task with the progress of your brand as well as any setbacks.

Step 2. Vision. I mentioned self-awareness first because understanding who you are will contribute greatly to how you view the remaining qualities of your brand. Initially it may seem that vision should be the first of the seven qualities and that notion is understandable because before you have an actual brand, you had to have the vision to develop the brand. I chose to make this the second quality because as I mentioned before, a bunch of jumbled ideas are chaotic in your head until you write them down, look at them as something other than just a dream, and then strategically develop those ideas into what is now a brand.

You did that with your SWOT analysis and a few other questions that you've answered along the way; so now we can come back to the vision because quite frankly, the vision never stops. The vision is a declaration of everything concerning your brand from the short-, medium-, and long-term goals, all the way down to who will join you on the journey (i.e. partners, employees, clients) and how you will travel the journey.

Successful brands always have a clear vision and they take the necessary steps to learn about options that are available in their industries and they also develop their own options based on where the industry is that they aspire to see. Let's take a look at Apple again. It is clear that Apple has vision because soon after the release of one product, we start to hear discussion about the next great product and all of the unbelievable features it will possess. Brands that lack vision find themselves playing "catch up" because they are trying to keep up with what others are doing rather than creating their own identity by setting the standard. Vision is always associated with leadership. Leaders are innovative; they have ideas and aspirations for their brands that others simply can't understand. Everyone is not a leader and that is OK, but in order to be an entrepreneur or the head of any business or corporation, leadership and vision are mandatory traits.

Step 3. Creativity. Vision and creativity seem synonymous but actually, they are only slightly similar. The vision should be implemented creatively but the visionary may not be the one to creatively implement that vision. For example, you may have a great idea for something as simple as a flyer, but you may not know how to implement that vision creatively. It may take the creativity of your business partner or your graphic designer, or even one of your employees. The point is to make sure that everything that happens with your company happens in a creative way. That is what will set you apart.

The most successful brands have figured out a way to be so creative with their products and services that they stand out among the competition. Not only are they creative with the launch of their brands, but they also maintain that creativity throughout the life of their brand.

Step 4. Relatable. Brands that are relatable are brands that have figured out the needs of their clients. Relatable simply means that you understand what your client wants and you perform accordingly based on their wants and needs.

When I worked for one of the largest public health systems in the southeast region, one of the initiatives was patient education. We wanted to educate patients about various diseases that were drastically affecting their demographic. Now the company had a website; it had annual reports, magazines, and all types of other methods of communication, but those methods were not effective for this particular client base. Remember, the clients in this case are patients and for a public hospital, the patients are, very generally speaking, lower income or indigent families. These families may not be able to view the health information on the Internet, because they may not have access to a computer or Internet and if they do it may not be regular access. Forget the Internet, they may not even have a home address; remember some of the patients are also homeless.

Nevertheless, as the brand that is deeply concerned about the health of this population, we had to find creative ways to communicate with our clients and be effective in that communication. Not only did we want them to have access to the information, but we also wanted them to understand it and respond accordingly to what they learned. We found the best way to do that was to develop a mobile outreach unit, which was basically a mobile bus that went directly to these areas with counselors, community volunteers and targeted communication, to talk to the people and help them understand the importance of doctor visits, or taking medication as prescribed. We also conducted health fairs and screenings in popular areas of these communities with doctors and nurses on site to provide medical care and education about health conditions both individually and community-wide.

This was a creative and realistic way to reach the audience. We couldn't sit back and wait for them to come to us because we understood that there were other variables preventing them from doing so, such as time, money, and transportation, so we went to them and it was always successful.

Your location, accessibility, pricing, language or verbiage, and approach should all be appropriate to your clients' availability. You can always expand your brand later to include different clients and when you do, that approach will be tailored specifically to them; but no matter the client, please make sure that you understand their likes, dislikes, and circumstances before you market to them.

Step 5. Visibility. I must admit that this is one quality that is extremely important to me, because it is the very essence of why my job exists. We publicists are devoted to helping our clients increase their visibility to their target audience. Even if you do not have a publicist yet, you should always strive to remain visible to your audience. Otherwise, how will they know you exist?

Visibility is not the same as vision, of course. Vision is what you see for your brand, visibility is solely about your clients seeing your brand and recognizing it when they do. I am going to pose two simple questions to help you determine ways to create your visibility. As always, write down your answers and act accordingly to the strengths and weaknesses of your answers.

1. Do your clients know how to find you? Do you have ways that they can stay updated with you, such as a store, website, social media accounts, commercials, media appearances, etc.? You may not be able to afford the outrageous expense of recurring radio and commercial spots, so how will you stay in the minds of the people who need your brand?

2. Are you physically visible at locations your clients frequently visit? I suppose that the first question should be, "Do you know where your clients are?" If not, do the research to find out because at this point, you should definitely know that answer.

Now when I say are "you" visible, I don't necessarily mean *you* per se (if you are not the brand); but is your brand visible at the locations of your clients? For example, if you are an athletic brand then is your brand where the athletes are? Events such as races, sporting events, health fairs, parks, recreational facilities, etc. are the perfect places to reach out to your clients if you are the owner of a sports shoe brand because those are the places where you will find your clients. **You can't wait for your audience to Google you and find your brand, you have to find them and introduce your brand.**

Top brands are always in the forefront. I like to run and I participate in a lot of 5 and 10Ks, and at these races, I always see certain bottled water companies, sports shoe brands, chiropractic clinics, and sporting goods stores represented at these races. Whether they are the sponsors or they just have flyers that they are passing out, they understand that the people they want to buy their products are at these events and subsequently, so are they.

Step 6. Sustainability.   We know that all of these qualities we are reviewing are important to the success of your brand. I know that you get that; but I would say that this one is also at the top of the list because at the end of the day, the goal of starting a business is to stay in business. Who wants to open a business just to shut it down in a few months or years? No one. Everything that we discuss in this book is to help your business thrive. Sustainability is the goal of every brand. You want to be the company that is trustworthy and has loyal clients who will stick by you, support your expansion, and support your mission for years to come.

I feel this way about Toyota and Lexus vehicles. In my world, there are not many brands available to the general population that compare to two these two brands (owned by the same company, by the way). I base my opinions about both cars on my own personal experiences. I was extremely pleased with the total package of the Lexus and Toyota experience and as a result, although there may be a better car out there, I'm not interested in finding out.   That's the trick to sustainability. If you can create loyal customers through trust, planning, product and brand alignment and all of the other qualities that we are discussing in this book, you will be able to sustain your business.

Sustainability involves being open to the change in your industry, being prepared for that change, and responding accordingly. The longer you are around, the more change you will experience. The key is to adjust to that change without compromising the objective of meeting the needs of your customers.

When we talk about product and brand alignment that basically means that your product or service is living up to the "hype" that you've created through branding. It's being true to your word and making sure that your product is exactly what you said it would be and more, in some cases. Think about companies that have proven sustainability and when you think about their brands, you will notice that in most cases the products that you considered have changed very little in their branding, but have grown and expanded with time, based on the trends of their industry.

Step 7. Translatable. This quality involves answering one question: Does it take a lot of energy to figure you out? I know that earlier I told you to be creative and unique, but don't be so abstract that no one understands what you do or for whom you do it. Think again about your favorite brands, why are they your favorite? What do they look like? How do they explain themselves? What do they say? If you really think about it, it doesn't take a rocket scientist to figure out these brands. Find a way to simplify your message and tailor that message specifically to your target audience. If you can't figure out how to do that then call me and I will be happy to help you do it.

Remember, the objective of all of your branding efforts is for people to "get you." Broken relationships always result in someone saying something such as, "he or she just doesn't understand me." Well your brand is the relationship between you and your clients and we want you all to have great communication. You need to know what they feel about you and they need to know how you want them to feel about you in addition to how you feel about them. If your audience is children, then everything about you should be kid-friendly. Don't worry about tailoring your brand to the parents because parents love whatever their child loves. Besides, if you are successful enough with your kid-friendly brand, there may be an avenue for an expanded brand that focuses on adults later down the road.

The Disney brand is the kid-friendly brand MVP. If you think about it, everything about Disney is catered towards youth but parents are still 100 percent on board with the Disney magic. Disney does not cater to the parents in hopes that they would translate to the kids. They promote directly to the kids, who in turn, go to their parents about their many, many, many, many, many, (did I mention many) wants and wishes as it relates to Disney.

So the moral of the story with this chapter is that with the myriad of brands that your customers are inundated with, standing out is your lifeline. Think of this as a similar process to applying for a job. Your resume doesn't hire you; it grabs the attention of the employer. After meeting you, the employer then determines if you get the job.

Your brand is your resume and the experience that the customer has with your brand is the interview. Employers receive multiple resumes on a daily basis and realistically, depending on the size of the organization, hiring managers cannot possibly read all of the resumes, in their entirety, that they receive. There is something about the selected resumes that stand out among the rest. Does your brand stand out? Why or why not? Can it stand out even more? How? You can start by staying compliant and mindful of the above characteristics and base your work on the results of your SWOT analysis.

I'm going to give you a small homework assignment for the end of the chapter. Yes, there is homework, because I want to make sure that if you get nothing else from this book, you get these seven qualities. They are the life and death of your brand. Think about your favorite brands, or even some of the brands that we have discussed, such as Apple, Nike, Chick-fil-A, Toyota, Lexus, or maybe you have your own favorite brands that come to mind. Pick two or three with one being a brand that is well known in your industry.

Do a little research on what these brands have communicated over the years. Look at their slogan, mission, community involvement, customer ratings, social media, website, logos, and everything else that we have talked about pertaining to branding. Do they possess the qualities that we have discussed in this chapter? If so, list the qualities and the ways they are presented in those companies. This will only provide you with a visual of the tactics that the successful and sustainable brands are using to continue longevity in their industry. If you are going to be the best, you must know how the best do it!

Chapter 8: Brand Identity

When Aria was born I had the perfect little outfits picked out for her to wear during her hospital stay and on the car ride home. God forbid that she wear those little hospital shirts that every other newborn was dressed in, during her first week of life! I picked out a week's worth of little newborn gowns in different colors with matching caps, mittens and booties and I couldn't wait to dress her in them.

She is going to love these little outfits! I thought, when I purchased them.
She is going to be a little baby superstar and love every minute of the attention. So I thought.

On the day that she was born, after we were all settled into our hospital room, I could not wait to dress her in her first little outfit. I quickly searched through the bag to see which one she would wear first. I found it! I changed her from the hospital gown into the cute little pink and brown newborn gown with the matching booties, mittens and cap. I laid her back down in her crib and got the camera ready to start snapping pictures. I am not exaggerating when I say that as long as it took me (which wasn't long at all) to lay her down, get the camera, and turn back towards her, the mittens, cap and one bootie were already off.

I fixed her garments and tried again. This time she wasn't able to slide out of the cap, which was too small for her head, but she was able to work those booties off. My perfect outfit was not going over as well as I thought. Pretty soon she started to get fussy and finally let out a very impressive cry for a person only four hours old.

As I got to know her more, I learned that she didn't do well with being restricted. She didn't like booties; hated mittens; and was irritated by caps. What I bought before I met her didn't match her personality and through no fault of her own, the entire set of gowns seemed three times too big and long for her. Needless to say, when I was pregnant I did not expect any of this when I envisioned her newborn look. Let me add this though, four years later, she loves hats and gloves, and anything that will make her look like a princess. My vision turned out not to be totally wrong, but my timing was definitely off. I needed to learn more about her personality before I could really dress her in a manner that fit who she really was.

This brings me to the reason for this chapter. It is time now to talk about what some may have expected this entire branding book to cover...the brand identity. After really analyzing and soul searching about your company's identity, you may have found that now your brand looks a little differently than what you originally expected. It's ok, that's not a bad thing. That simply means that you have realistically analyzed what your company can and will offer to your clients. You've also completed a SWOT analysis that should have revealed a few new ideas and possibilities either short or long term.

Prior to this analysis, you were looking at the company through the lens of an ultrasound. You thought you knew what your baby looked like, but it was only from a very limited perspective. Now that you have given birth and you've really analyzed the company's identity, you can dress your baby according to its personality.

My outfits for Aria were slightly off because I didn't know her as an actual person yet. I determined her "look" based on my vision for her and not on who she actually turned out to be. Don't get me wrong, that's not a bad thing because I had to start somewhere. I certainly wouldn't want to be at the hospital with no clothes for my newborn baby. It's just that it wasn't until I learned who she really was that I could match her look with her personality.

That is the point of brand identity. Like me, you have envisioned your baby from the moment it was conceived; it's not until you actually birth it however, that you can really determine its identity. As I mentioned, Aria turned out to be too big for the caps and too small for the gowns; while the booties and mittens didn't match her personality at all. When you were conceiving your brand, you had big plans for the brand identity but perhaps now that the brand is birthed and you are more in tune with its personality, you find that your brand may be too small for some aspects and too big for others; maybe the colors and preliminary designs don't fit at all with its actual personality. As a new parent to your brand, you had a lot of ideas and visions prior to its birth but now that it is here, you can really see what your brand should look like.

Brand identity is basically the tangible, visual aspects of your brand. Remember the brand is the personality/reputation while the brand identity is the visual demonstration of that. In its broadest definition, this includes the logo, website, color scheme, font, and communication of the brand that you've developed. I chose to cover brand identity at this point in the book because it is so important to first have a good understanding of your brand before you begin to "dress" it.

You are new parents and just as with any new parents, you went into this venture with a lot of emotions. On one hand, you thought you had some aspects of the business all figured out, while on the other hand there was a lot of uncertainty. It wasn't until slightly into the pregnancy and definitely after the birth that you realized that some adjustments were necessary. Hopefully at this point you are working on those adjustments and now feel more comfortable with the brand you are creating.

So let's talk about your brand identity. I'm going to give you two words to remember: consistent and intentional. When you are consistent, people remember you. Think of consistency as repetition. What's one of the most effective ways of learning? Repetition? If a person does something, or hears and reads something consistently, they retain the information. If your name changes every two years, or you start out with two different logos, or one day your logo is red and the next week it is blue that shows a lack of consistency. Especially when first starting out, your logo, colors, slogan and look should be consistent. Before I jump ahead to all of those let's take them one by one.

Logo design: One thing is for sure. Every business should have a name and a logo. Even if you use a unique font reflecting your business name then that's your logo. Take for example, Coca Cola, FedEx, and Disney. All of those are well known brands with recognizable logos. Their logos stand out because of the font and color scheme they use. Both are also always consistent. I would also like to point out that this idea works best with businesses with shorter names or acronyms.

If you notice, Coca-Cola is also called "Coke;" while FedEx was formerly known as Federal Express, and of course Walt Disney World is affectionately known as Disney. In a time when everything is instant and shorter, a company nickname or acronym is not a bad idea. Sometimes during rebranding, businesses with longer names shorten their names to reflect what's popular with their audience.

Take KFC for instance. At one time this famous chicken restaurant was known solely as Kentucky Fried Chicken. I'm not sure when it happened but one day I looked up and everyone was calling it KFC. I say that I'm not sure when, because the rebranding of the restaurant was so seamless that I'm not sure that people even realized that it was rebranded. I remember signs having both Kentucky Fried Chicken and KFC on them, and then the messaging started to identify as KFC and the next thing I realized, one day Kentucky Fried Chicken was gone and KFC was everywhere. This is what I mean when I say that as a brand you must change with the industry and trends, when appropriate.

We live in a time when everything is shortened. Do you remember back when JLO was Jennifer Lopez and MJ was actually Michael Jackson? We live in an instant society and everything we do and say must occur within seconds. Unless there is a justifiable reason why your business name must be an entire sentence long (and there aren't many reasons), try to find a way to shorten the name so that it is distinct and the service is clear.

Everything about your business should be clear. When you are designing your logo, it's best to make it relatable to the company name. The Nike swoosh can stand-alone now because at one point anytime you saw the name Nike, you saw the swoosh. As consumers, we know that a Nike shoe is not a Nike shoe unless it has the swoosh somewhere on it. If you are going to have a symbol as part of your logo, make sure that your business name is visible as well so that your audience can associate the symbol with the name of your organization.

Color Scheme: Your color scheme should be reflected in your logo. Now there are a few exceptions to this rule because you also have to think about how your logo will look on billboards and television, in black and white or color, or on ads or placements with different color backgrounds. I always recommend that unless you are a graphic designer, you should invest in the services of a graphic designer to help you think through color options and certain designs for your logo.

Graphic designers work with printers throughout the majority of their business, so they understand what works best where color and design are concerned. Does your logo still look as effective in black and white? There will be times when your logo will be printed in black and white and again, you want a consistent look so that whether black and white or color, multi or solid colored background, your logo still looks like your logo.

Graphic designers can also help you with identifying the most effective colors for your business. If you are opening a spa, you would not want your color scheme to include fire engine red, neon green or another bold color. Those colors contradict the intent of a spa. A spa should be serene and calm; it should be soothing and peaceful. The colors that I described earlier are the complete opposite of that. If you aren't sure what the colors for your brand should be, research the different emotions associated with certain colors as a start. Just because red is your favorite color personally doesn't mean that it should be the primary color of your spa's logo. Soothing colors are milder and less bold. Try to think of colors that spark your own emotions and build off of that.

Logo Placement: You may not realize it but logo placement on your deliverables such as letterhead, brochures, flyers, advertisements, all fall under the idea of consistency through brand identity. When I worked in healthcare our logo was always placed at the top left of any communication that we issued. The logo also had to be a certain font size and could only be altered after the approval of the public relations team.

Some may think this is excessive but it's actually the standard in corporate America and I think that all businesses should adopt this type of strategic thinking when it comes to their logo. Think of it this way, your logo is your social security number, so to speak. It's unique to you, no one else has it and anytime it is used, it directly affects you. Think of how protective we are about our social security numbers:

- We are advised not to carry the social security cards around in our wallets for fear that if it is stolen; the culprit has access to everything.
- We are cautious of who we share our number with and who is around when we share it.
- We destroy all older documents that include the number so that no one will find it.

Your logo should be viewed the same way. If your logo is associated with the wrong message, the effects could be detrimental to your brand. If it is misrepresented in the wrong way, you are the one who will have to do damage control. If it is affiliated with causes or organizations that directly contradict with your brand then you are the one viewed as dishonest and that is why, especially with a personal brand, you want to protect your logo in the same manner that you would protect your social security number.

Website and deliverables: Edit. Edit. Edit. As a writer, I cannot tell you how much emphasis I really want to put on this editing topic. Typos and errors say a lot about your company. Even if you are not a writer, or your product or services have nothing to do with writing, recurring errors and misspellings on your own site send a message of carelessness.

Trust me, I get it; with the great auto-correct invention that exists today, sometimes your computer or smartphone turns your perfectly correct word into something that you never intended. The correction sometimes happens so fast that you don't even realize that it happened. Nonetheless, you must take the time to proofread everything and then have an extra pair of eyes look at it. I would suggest preferably a professional or someone skilled at grammar and writing. If you are the person in charge of developing the content then you should definitely NOT be the person editing the work. It's really challenging to edit long pieces that you've developed yourself. In the rare case that you cannot find a content editor or proofreader for your website or written communication, here are a few tips to increase the chances of more accurate self-editing:

1. Edit the document from the end to the beginning – I do this before I pass along a written piece to someone else for editing. If you start at the end of the document and read it going forward, you are better able to catch misspelled words, because

your brain is not anticipating the natural next word. It works; trust me.

2. Edit a few days after you have finished the draft – I would not recommend that you try to edit a document yourself immediately after you've drafted it. One reason is that you are probably mentally fatigued from developing the content and can't give the document the attention that editing requires. You've given a lot of thought to what you want to say and how you want to say it. Taking a break for a couple of days will allow you to switch from the writer hat, to the editor hat. Another thing that happens if you don't detach is that you start editing for content and basically end up rewriting the document, rather than editing for grammar and usage.

3. Read aloud while editing – This sounds and feels a little silly but sometimes actually hearing the content aloud helps you to pinpoint errors.

It is so important that in addition to editing, your website and deliverables should do the following:

- **Exist!:** In 2015 you are *not* a credible business if you do not have a website. Although social media can sometimes be more comprehensive with rapid updates, it should never replace a website. After you have figured out your brand, logo, and services, the next step is the development of your website. If you are not at the point of hiring a web developer or web team, there are sites such as Godaddy.com and Wordpress.com, along with many others that will provide templates for you to create your own site.

The mandate here is to have something available where people can find out more about you, your company, your services, and a contact number for additional questions. If you have nothing else on your site at this point, at least have those main elements and anything else that is specific to your industry and company. Put yourself in your clients' shoes. What would YOU want to know about this company if you were a potential customer?

- **Inform:** As I just mentioned, the purpose of the website is to provide the potential client with detailed information about you and the business. The website has to cover the basics of your business. The client first needs to know who you are. I mean you, the owner.

  o What is your background, experience, and education, or any other relevant information that makes you credible enough to have a business doing what you do?

  o What is your business and why was it founded? This information introduces you to your client but also digs deeper into the purpose of the business. If your business is a non-profit that caters to at-risk youth and you explain that at one time you too were an at-risk youth, the client has learned about you on a deeper level. That information could be the difference between the selection of your non-profit and the competition.

  o What type of products or services do you provide? Be specific. This is not a 30 second commercial, social media, or a flyer; this is your opportunity to explain your services and why they are important.

o   What are your fees? Some sites choose not to list their fees but you should at least have information about how clients can reach you to receive a quote or discuss fees in person.

o   How can the customer connect with you? List your social media accounts, emails and any other method of communication under this tab. You can have the best product in the world, but if no one knows how to obtain it, all we have talked about is in vain.

o   What samples or photos of your work can you display? People want proof that you are who you say you are. If you are a musician and you have photos performing at different events, this is the area to share those photos. Videos are a plus. If you have video of past interviews that you have participated in, display them. Any sample of your work that you can provide should be included in a tab.

- **Engage:** Remember this: social media is important because it should drive people to your website, not replace your website. If you are not careful, social media can cause you to neglect your website. This happens because with social media you post a picture or video and you instantly likes or comments, and you can even respond back. That's great but you also want to make sure people are heading over to your home, your website. If you are a retailer with an online store, you definitely want to drive customers to your site because that's where they will see your merchandise.

Your social media accounts should always encourage people to visit the site and once they do, you have to make sure that the site looks and feels differently at each visit. People stop visiting websites when they realize that nothing about the site ever changes. If the same pictures, the same quotes, and the same information is there for months at a time, then why should your customer come back?

Now you can link your website with your social media so that the updates on social media also transfers over to the webpage. Create a calendar for new pictures and content. You can start a blog and have people visit your website to read your blog. Whatever the tactic is, it is important that you train your clients to check in with you at your website.

- **Motivate:** Your website should motivate your customer to take some type of action as it pertains to your business. Whether they book you for an event, or buy your product, at the end of the visit, there should be some type of motivation to connect with you further.

At the end of the business day, your brand and brand identity are a direct lifeline to the success of your business. I don't want your claim to fame to be that you are "the best kept secret!" If you are the best then it definitely should not be a secret. Everyone needs to know about you, especially your potential clients. All of the components we have discussed are directly connected to your brand. The brand that aligns with the brand identity and the product or service itself, are a match made in heaven.

Chapter 9: **You Are Your First Investor**

Children are expensive! Sorry... but there was no delicate way to say that. A lot of time, energy, and money are spent preparing for a child and parenting that child. It all starts the very moment that the child is conceived. Parents start purchasing cribs, decorating the new babies' rooms, they must have the latest and greatest strollers along with car seats, diapers, bottles, and of course, clothes. Although baby showers are extremely helpful, the parents-to-be still wind up purchasing additional wants and needs for their children.

Let's not even begin to discuss how the mother-to-be has to watch her body grow and expand at an uncomfortably alarming rate over a period of 40 weeks. There is no question that a wardrobe budget is all but a mandate to accommodate her rapid growth. Doctor visits, maternity photos, and perhaps even additional parenting and birthing classes are other incidentals to add to the spending chart. Remember, this is just the pregnancy; the baby hasn't even arrived yet! The financial responsibility doesn't end at the delivery of the baby; however, oh no, the fun has just begun.

According to an article in the March 18, 2014, Personal Finance section of Forbes Magazine, contributor Laura Shin points out that,

> A child born in 2012 will cost his parents $241,080 in 2012 dollars, on average, over his lifetime. And children of higher-earning families drain the bank account more: Families earning more than $105,000 annually can expect to spend $399,780 per child.

I don't know about you, but to me, that sounds like a major investment—and that's just monetarily! Children, whether during pregnancy or post-partum, also require a tremendous amount of energy and attention. Expecting parents spend their time and energy thinking about the pregnancy and the baby. New parents spend their time and energy trying to learn how to parent, and experienced parents spend their time and energy actually parenting. The investments never stop because the parenting experience is that of a roller coaster ride: scary, thrilling, exhilarating, rewarding, and all consuming! Guess what? It's all worth it.

The time, energy, and financial resources that you put towards your child, truly are investments that never stop. I can admit that no matter what I am doing throughout the day, my thoughts are always on my daughter. What is she doing at school? Did she take a nap? What will I prepare for dinner? Did I remember to tell her to have a good day? Will I do something that will cause her to require the services of a therapist later in life? From the most miniscule thought to the most elaborate thought, I am always thinking about ways to help her learn, grow, and develop.

Then there is the actual attention that she needs from her father and me. Children need the attention of their parents and parents need to be attentive to their children in order to fully understand the children's needs. My daughter loves my attention. Whether she is telling me about her day or wants us to play dolls together, she enjoys one-on-one time. Let me rephrase that, she enjoys my undivided attention and when she has it, I am better able to understand her thoughts, behavior, actions, and overall personality, because we had an encounter. It's not just about playing together and doing fun things, as a parent, your attention should also focus on the child's growth, development, behavior, health, and everything else that makes that child who he or she has become.

I know you are saying, "I did not buy this book to talk about parenting," but stick with me here because this will all make sense in just a moment. My point is that just as a parent must invest in their child, you must invest in your brand! It is your baby after all. I want the absolute best for my daughter, but it will take more than just *wanting* the best. As her parent, along with my husband, we must actively and completely invest in her in order to see the results that we hope for. The same is true concerning the investment you make in your brand. If you want to attain your goals, the primary investor in your company must be you.

Although this topic is not directly related to public relations and branding, I feel that it is important to mention the fact that in order to start a business, you must be willing to invest in your business. I mentioned the parenting aspect because the principles are the same. Your brand needs your time and energy, attention, and finances in order to grow. Sure we would all love to have a private investor take an interest in our business and fund all of our needs. That is an ideal and pretty unrealistic expectation, but it sounds great! The bottom line is that before anyone else will put one dime towards your brand or even donate one second of their time, you must show by your own commitment that it is worth the investment.

I've conducted a few workshops and participated in a few panel discussions throughout my career and one statement that always comes up and always frustrates me to no end is when, during the question and answer portion, someone says, "I can't find anyone to believe in my business. What do I do now?" It never fails. That statement always pops up by an attendee and they are looking at the panelist for the magic answer. My answer is always in the form of this question, "Do YOU believe in your business? The attendee will usually respond affirmatively, which leads me to say, "Well then you've found your one."

All it really takes to start your business is you. You make the first investment. You do the necessary work to get it started. You put the time, energy, and money towards the foundation. You do all of that because at the end of the day, no one is as passionate about your business as you. Even those supporters with the best intentions for you are not and should not be more passionate about your business than you. I say should not because if you are not the most passionate person out there about your brand, then why are you pursuing it?

If you are not willing to invest the necessary resources into your brand, then what is your true motivation for starting your business? I would like to just take one moment to make this statement: **If money is your motivation for doing what you do, then stop right now and close up shop.**

Of course we all want to be profitable in our businesses, that's a no-brainer but the ultimate purpose of your company, business, brand, personal brand, whatever you want to call it, should not be solely motivated by the desire to make money. Why, you ask? I'll tell you; if money is your sole motivation, then when you don't have the money, you are no longer motivated. On the other hand, if money is your sole motivation, then when you make a reasonable portion of money, it's also easy to lose the motivation. For an entrepreneur, the passion behind your business should stem from the aspects that we discussed earlier. What was your personal reason for starting your business? What life, educational, or other experience led you to want to do what you do?

I was always told that you know you have a passion to do something, when you experience the same satisfaction doing your passion for free as you would if you were being paid to do it. Here's another thought related to that: If you are willing to do your passion for free, simply because you love doing it, then it is truly a passion. Now I am not saying that you should start your business and perform your services at no cost. That would definitely not be sound advice. We don't live in a world where we can afford to work for free and I get that but my point is that when you chose to do what you do, your motivation should have been that you enjoy doing whatever "it" is so much that you wouldn't mind also getting paid for it.

Having said that, let's go back to your investment. When you are passionate about something you are willing to do what is necessary to make it work at its best. As it relates to your child, if you are passionate about your child then you don't mind investing in a tutor to help her or him improve scholastically. You don't mind paying to register your child for football or cheerleading. You don't mind staying up all night nursing a sick child back to good health. You don't mind taking the day off of work to have lunch with your child at school or volunteer in his or her class. Why? You don't mind because you are passionate about your child and all of these investments will have a positive outcome.

Business experts call this concept the return on investment or ROI. The return on investment is simply the profit that you receive back from what you have invested. Investing your time, attention, and finances toward your child during the formative years will have a great return when they are successful and thriving adults. The same goes for your business; investing your time, attention, and finances toward your brand will reap a great return on investment when others are ready to invest also and you begin to see the fruit of your labor.

In the past few chapters, I mentioned a few situations where the services of a professional may be needed to help you set a solid foundation for your business. I've mentioned lawyers, publicists, web designers, writers, and editors. Now trust me, I understand that when you are a new entrepreneur, you can't necessarily budget for the services of all of these professionals. I understand that usually a new or emerging entrepreneur may have serious financial limitations, but again, the first investment starts with the entrepreneur. In this case, it starts with you. You may not be able to afford the services of a business lawyer when you first research or reach out to one to learn of their fees, but after you find out how much it will cost; you save for it.

No one ever said that you have to start your business the next day after you conceive it. In fact, I recall that in one of the first chapters in this book, I mentioned that the pregnancy stage can take as long or as little as you need. Think of it this way: What do you call a birth that happens too soon? Premature. Although advances are made every day to reduce the number of premature births and increase the survival rates of these births, they are still happening. No parent wants to experience a premature birth. The development of the fetus is so strategic and timely that at least 39 of the entire 40 weeks is necessary for the full development to occur. The effects of premature births can be lasting and yes, progress has definitely been made to eliminate or reduce some of the lasting implications of premature births, but ideally every parent would rather their baby develop to full term.

The same goes for your brand. Although the conception phase was rewarding, you have to have patience during the pregnancy and make sure that your brand is able to fully develop before you give birth. The survival of a business is difficult as it is. You don't want to add to that difficulty by rushing into business prematurely before you are ready to deliver. If there is something that you need to make your business better then go for it. Plan, research, and save until you have the appropriate funds or resources available to obtain what will make your business even better.

I'd like to add that even after you birth your brand, you may have to slow the process or make some necessary adjustments before you take the next step; and that's ok. You aren't on anyone's timeline. You want to have your foundation set and solid before you move too fast and have the entire project crumble due to lack of preparation. So take your time and save; or realistically coordinate how you will make the investments that are needed for your business to move forward. By no means should you wait on anyone!

My advice to you is to figure out which of the above professional services that I mentioned are the priority for where are right now. After you figure that out spend the time, energy, or money to hire that professional to help you with that part of the process. If you need to consult with a business lawyer because you just don't understand some of the legal aspects of starting a business, then by all means find a good lawyer, find out their fees, save the money, and hire that lawyer. The last thing you want to do is to end up in a legal bind that will cost triple the amount to get out of, than it would have to seek counsel. **It is way more expensive to hire someone to fix your**

problem than it is to hire someone who will help prevent the problem.

I feel that it is important to also point out that if you do hire a lawyer, you don't necessarily need to hire them on a retainer. A retainer is usually a flat fee for unlimited services monthly. You may only need to pay a lawyer for a consultation, then afterwards you can file the appropriate paperwork based on their recommendation. You may hire them just for a contractual period. For example, if you need a legal professional to help you through the entire establishment of a business, then you may need to only hire the lawyer for a contractual period of three months, depending on your needs. My point is that you should be willing to invest and do so according to your immediate needs.

I'll talk about this in the upcoming chapter, but the same goes for a publicist. A beginning entrepreneur who just received their business license yesterday does not need to hire me as their publicist. That would be a waste of money as well as time and energy on both of our parts because there are so many other more pressing needs to be met before the services of a publicist are needed.

What I would recommend is that the entrepreneur hire me for guidance on developing their brand. For a flat rate a PR professional will guide you, in more detail, through the steps that we've discussed for developing your brand. I would also help develop a strategic communications plan, revise any deliverables such as bios, fact sheets, etc., or provide content editing services for documents, and websites. The list could go on and on, but the point is that you invest in the services that you need for that point in the process so that everything looks professional and you have someone skilled who can guide you through the process.

The next item on the agenda for this chapter is perfecting your craft. No one knows everything. In order to stay competitive you must be willing to learn and grow. We talked about your investment being than just financial; you must also invest ample time and attention to your brand. This means that you cannot get the business up and running and then just "go with the flow" and see what happens. You have to pay attention to your brand. What is happening in the industry? Are you familiar with the latest trends and technological advances? Is there a new social media movement that your competition has mastered, but you aren't quite up to speed? Maybe it has just been a while since you received your formal education about your industry and things are just changing. These and other potential situations may arise and before they do you have to stay ahead in order to compete.

Paying attention to the trends by joining professional organizations in your field or attending conferences, workshops, networking events are all just as vital to your success as the work you put forth to start the business. You can always be better at what you do; and with colleges and universities releasing the next generation of leaders in your field who are already ahead of the curve, it's important to continue to get better. Don't despise the learning process. You owe it to your brand, your clients and yourself to stay knowledgeable of everything there is to know concerning your business.

Again, I understand that starting out, you won't be able to necessarily travel the world attending conference after conference or every workshop or seminar that is out there. I do understand that. That's why you get creative. That's where the time and energy investments come in.

You have to put forth the time and energy to find ways to continue to learn even if you don't have the finances to do so. Does your favorite brand or business organization host webinars? If so, that is a great option, because unless the webinar is free, the only cost would be registration. You have instantly saved money by avoiding airfare, hotel stay, extra meal costs and all other travel expenses.

Can you afford to go back to school to get an advanced degree? If so, go for it! If not, consider enrolling in a class or two at the local college or university? Most schools now have a continuing education department that hosts evening classes on a wide range of subjects. Investing in the local graphic design course through the continuing education department may teach you the basic skills you need for developing creative flyers or brochures. By investing $299 for the course, you are actually saving close to triple that amount by learning the skill yourself and eliminating the need to hire a graphic designer for every project.

When considering any investment, you should always base your decision on the return on that investment.

Why are the brand examples we have discussed throughout the book still so successful? They have stayed ahead of their industry by investing whatever was necessary to achieve the ultimate goal of business success. You have never heard anyone say, "Apple is so behind the times;" or "I'm so tired of the same Starbucks flavors!" Whether you like Apple and Starbucks or not, you have to admit that part of their success is they are able to stay ahead of the competition. You can do that also, even with limited resources. All it takes is for you to develop your investment plan.

I know. I know. You're thinking, "Here she goes again with the questions and answers!" You're absolutely right. This book is designed to condition you to think strategically and dig deeper into aspects of your business that will make it successful. I am going to give you a few questions to help you decide whether a particular opportunity is worth the investment:

- **What are my goals for the brand?** You should already know the answer to this question in a broader sense, but this pertains specifically to the short term, more immediate goals of the brand.

For instance, your goal may be to increase your social media following or perhaps to become a registered business in your state.

- **How immediate or vital is this goal to achieving the next step in my business?** If your goal is to become a registered business, that's a pretty pressing goal. Not achieving this goal definitely places a major barrier in front of other items on your to do list. Prioritize your goal and weigh the value of the opportunity to potentially meet that goal.

- **Will this potential opportunity help or hurt my chances of reaching the desired goal?** This is pretty self-explanatory. Ask yourself, "How much closer to my goals will I be because of this possible opportunity?" Not every opportunity is appropriate for your brand. Be very thoughtful and strategic when determining which opportunities to take. After careful planning and counsel, if the opportunity seems beneficial, take it!

- **If I do not invest in this opportunity, how will that impact or delay achieving my goal?** If you need to seek a lawyer to help you set up your business and you don't do that, the potential impact could be that you either miss a vital step in the process, or that you further delay starting your business.

- **Do I have resources readily available to help me with this opportunity?** Whether it is money, skills, experience, contacts, or the availability of certain products or services, take a good look at what you already have to work with and assess its potential impact on the steps toward your goals.

- **Are there any other opportunities that may be more attainable that will achieve the same desired result?** You may not be able to afford, right now, the best graphic designer in the country; however, there may be graphic design students who need course credit or an internship. These are the perfect resources to use, because they are knowledgeable, inexpensive and in most cases utilize the guidance of their instructors.

The key is that no matter the opportunity; if it is too far beyond your current reach, think of alternative ways to continue to get the job done.

- **What are the barriers to pursuing this opportunity and how can I overcome them?** This is a deeper analysis of the previous question. Think specifically about your barriers and write down as many creative ways as you can think of to overcome them. The strongest quality of an entrepreneur is tenacity. Continue to press towards your goals no matter the obstacle.

- **What will be the return on my investment?** *"If I pay to attend this conference, I may sell x number of products and make a profit." "If I go to this networking event, I may increase my social media followers by x." "If I attend this webinar, I may learn how to enhance my ability to perform my service."* Whatever the case may be, focus on the end return rather than the immediate cost. This is your business and you want to move ahead and achieve success, so you must be willing to make the initial investment.

The list could go really go on and on, but I look at these questions as the core that will help you analyze whether it is appropriate to invest time, attention, or finances into a particular opportunity. Perform the simple task of weighing the pros and cons. If you find that the opportunity has benefits, then by all means, go for it. Take the necessary measures whether it's sacrificing one expense to pay for your brand investment, saving the money to meet the cost of the investment, or perhaps losing a little sleep or energy to attend night classes to improve your skills. Whatever the case may be, **your brand will only be as successful as the time and energy you are willing to expend.** Get to work!

Chapter 10: **Work**

"The only place success comes before work is in the dictionary." –Vince Lombardi

I titled this chapter Work, because that's one word that needs no introduction. Just as the above quote suggests if you want to achieve your dreams, you must work for them. This journey demands hard work. There is no way around it; but what I would like to discuss here are the different aspects of work and the difficult work-related questions that all entrepreneurs must face. Do I quit my full time job and dive right into this business? How long do I stay at my fulltime job when starting a new business? I've quit my job, now what? Will I ever rest again? If you haven't experienced these questions and probably a few others similar, then don't worry, you will. So I will try to provide some insight to help you think clearly about the answers to these questions.

Are you a stay-at-home parent? I mean are you at a point where your business is your fulltime job? If so, I like to call that stay-at-home parenting. Why? Because you are able to focus your attention solely on developing your business with no pressure to commit to a full-time employer. This is quite similar to the responsibility of a stay-at-home parent to children. They are able to fully commit to the growth and development of their children with no pressure from the responsibilities of a full time job. To some, this sounds like such an easy task. I've heard so many people say that if they didn't have the barrier of a full time job and could just stay at home and work or parent, their lives would be so much simpler. Well, I am not a stay-at-home parent in either sense (business or personal) but I do feel qualified to say that although it sounds desirable, there is nothing simple about solely parenting your child or your business.

I mean really, the point of starting your own business is to be your own boss. Who wants to be the boss in one setting and then have a boss in the other? The goal of every entrepreneur is to be able to do what they enjoy doing, full time. This is your goal as well, I'm sure. If it were not, then you probably wouldn't have started your own business. I want to help you figure out how to make the additional employment, or lack thereof, work in your favor, and also help you learn to find a work-life balance while on this journey of entrepreneurship.

I admire stay-at-home parents both figuratively and literally. For parents of children, the task requires the ability to multi-task while exhibiting a great deal of patience and flexibility. It is an extremely tough job that some misinterpret as a luxury. Even if the parent of a child does not desire to stay at home completely full time, every parent appreciates a work-life balance where they are able to attend to the needs of their children freely. It's not a job for the faint of heart by any means, and neither is parenting your business full time or part time.

Although stay at home parents of a brand are able to devote a lengthier amount of time to their business than someone who works for an employer full-time, there is still a great deal of pressure, sacrifice, and motivation required to stay committed to your brand when it is your sole or primary income. In an earlier chapter I talked about how money can't be the motivation for starting your business, because when the money is not present, neither is the motivation. Well this is the perfect example of a time when as a business owner, you have to let your passion for your industry drive your motivation. When you have to downsize your lifestyle or heaven forbid lose certain luxuries or even necessities because of your business's initial lack of adequate income, how do you maintain motivation? Those who are truly passionate and genuine about their desires for their businesses are able to stay motivated even when the circumstances look bleak.

I worked with two clients with similar stories of work ethic. Both quit their jobs in corporate America to pursue their dreams of entrepreneurship. Both struggled financially, downsized significantly, and poured all of their energies and resources into starting their business. One client, Client A already possessed the skills that she needed for her business. She always had the desire to utilize her skill to start her own business. She started her business from scratch, used the resources that were available to her such as skill, equipment, etc. and found her place in her industry. Ten years later, although her strive toward greatness has never ended, she has achieved a measurable amount of success in her field.

She did not quit and even though there were many difficult times, she stayed committed to being a stay-at-home parent to her brand, and eventually reaped the benefits.

Client B also left her very successful corporate job to start her business. Unlike Client A, she didn't readily know where her path would lead, but she knew that the corporate environment was not her destination. She quit her job, went on a sabbatical, and did a lot of soul searching to really analyze her life's purpose. Finally, she figured it out. She realized that her interests and hobbies were really her passion and calling. So she moved to another state where she felt that her business would thrive, invested in her business and now nearly 10 years later is also very well known in her industry and successful at what she does. The work ethic and motivation kept her committed to her decision to focus solely on her new career and it also paid off very well for her.

Both of these women worked hard to build their brands. They are recognized in their industries as sustainable brands. I won't get too detailed into their stories, because I have a feeling that they both will have their own books out very soon, but what I will say is that there comes a point where you must be willing to sacrifice in order to be rewarded.

Why am I telling you this? It's because everyone's story is different but the message is always the same. Hard work pays off. You may not be at the point of stay-at-home parenting right now, but that doesn't mean it won't ever happen. It may take a while before you are at that point, but embrace where you are now and deal with it accordingly. Some of you reading this book may have to work a full time or part-time job in order to sustain, while you start your business and that's ok if you do. That's my story. I am a working mother and a working entrepreneur and that's what works best for me.

I live in a neighborhood filled with stay-at-home moms. As I pull out of my garage every morning, I am always greeted with the hearty smiles and waves goodbye from moms going on their morning jogs while pushing her children in the stroller. Doesn't that sound just lovely! I wave back happily and head out on my way to work. When I first went back to work after having Aria;

however, I was extremely upset that I couldn't stay at home with her the way these moms were able to do. The hardest thing for a new mom to do is leave her child to go back to work. I wanted to take her on morning jogs and experience all of her firsts the same way the other moms in the neighborhood were able to do. I realized later that their story was just not my story. My story was that I worked full time, parented full time, and was in the process of starting my own business. Crazy huh?

My point is that I did not let any of my circumstances stop me from my goals. I wanted to excel at my full time job, break the record for parenting success, and start my own business so that one day I would solely be my full time employer. Today as I write, that is still my desire and through my sacrifices I see the return on my investments both in business and parenting. I'm saying this to you to say that there is never a perfect time to start your business. There is never a perfect time to leave your job, if that's what you have to do. There is never a perfect situation with anyone no matter how perfect it looks; the key is to embrace your journey and respond accordingly to your life's situations.

I would like to point out that although I was never a stay-at-home mom, I experienced all of Aria's firsts and instead of morning jogs with the stroller, we took evening jogs with the stroller which was a great de-stressor after a long day's work. I have found a balance between work, work, (yes, I know that I said it twice but I have two jobs, remember?) and parenting, with the understanding that at any given time, the priority can shift. When it does, the response is to simply respond. When it is time to leave my full-time and allow my business to become full-time, I will know and respond. The main objective that I want you to understand here is that you have to recognize when it's time to respond and when it is, simply take the appropriate steps to respond accordingly.

So when do I respond? When is it time to step out and become a stay-at-home parent to my business? I hear you asking me this and the truthful answer is that I don't know. I can't tell you that. What I can tell you is this: when it is time, you will know. Ideally, the time is when the income and success from your secondary job outweighs that of your primary job. In other words when your own business gets to the point that you are sustainable enough to do it solely. Others might argue that the time may be when your commitment to your employer becomes a hindrance to your entrepreneurial goals. Either could be the case for you, but what you need to remember is that you will know the best response for your unique situation.

In the meantime, there is another issue at hand. You are working full time, starting a business, trying to have a social life, trying to manage a family, oh; and you may want to sleep occasionally as well. Truthfully, whether you are a stay-at-home parent or an independent business owner, any of these circumstances could apply. One thing is constant for both types of entrepreneurs: the hard work that you put forth can become extremely overwhelming and when it does, it is time to initiate balance. Actually balance should have been initiated from the beginning when you were doing your SWOT analysis, but since we were so focused on developing that brand at that time, we can go ahead and incorporate it now.

I would like to provide you with a few tips to help you reduce stress and establish a work-life balance.

1. **Think of your full-time job as your investor:** So you've searched for an investor, right? If you haven't I'm sure that you've dreamed of the day that you would have one. Well, you've found one! If you are receiving a steady weekly or monthly paycheck from an employer, then think of them as your investor for your business. Your additional income can be used to eliminate some of the financial strain that comes with starting a business. With effective budgeting and planning you can use some of that income, even if it is only every now and then, to help you fund some of your entrepreneurial goals.

   Look at it this way; because you do have an income stream, you can budget in (where possible) some of the priority tasks that you have to accomplish. I understand that times can get tough, especially for an entrepreneur, but remember the return on investment will reap great rewards. Put yourself in someone else's shoes and think about that entrepreneur who does not have an income other than their business, but still has the same goals as you.

Where they may or may not have to look for additional employment to supplement their income, you already have it. Use it wisely and it can serve the same purpose as an actual investor.

If you are a stay-at-home parent, you may have to consider part-time, seasonal, or contractual work to help you offset some of the expenses that you may incur with your business. You know your situation better than anyone and in no way am I advising you to return to full-time employment outside of your business, but I am advising that you make the necessary sacrifices to help you achieve your entrepreneurial goals. A part-time job, increasing your business rates (where applicable), or downsizing your current lifestyle to save money for branding needs are some suggestions. These are the sacrifices that are required to be successful at what you do. These are suggestions to help alleviate some of the strain that can present itself when starting a business. If you work hard now, you can definitely play harder later.

2. **Pace Yourself:** You may not know this about me, but I am an amateur runner. I started running a few years ago and haven't looked back. When I first started running, I didn't quite understand the science behind it and I just ran until I couldn't go any further. Instead of progressing, it seemed as though I was just spinning my wheels so to speak. My running goal when I first started was to "not stop." There was no strategy behind my running; I just ran. Well it wasn't until adhering to the advice of a running coach that I learned that I needed to pace myself in order to be the most productive.

   Pacing is maintaining a realistic speed in order to ultimately accelerate from the start to finish line as effectively as possible. If a runner starts the race too fast, he or she will run out of "gas" before finishing. If the runner starts out too slowly he or she may waste too much time getting to the finish line, resulting in a slower race time. Pacing however, involves understanding your destination and adjusting appropriately based on how fast your body is able to move.

That same concept applies to your business moves. It is important to move at YOUR pace; keep moving and finish. Pacing yourself helps to achieve these goals because everything that is happening is happening at your pace. If you are a new entrepreneur with a makeup line, your line will not be able to operate the same way as CoverGirl...initially.   Moving at your own pace based on *your* capabilities will keep you in the race while moving too fast or too slowly could ultimately disqualify you.

How can I move too fast in my business you ask? There are plenty of ways: you could hire a full staff before you have the adequate resources and funds to support them and your business. This type of move could end in bankruptcy. Another could be spending money to advertise to your audience before you have the supply in place to meet the demand. What good is advertising during radio's peak hours when you don't even have the staff or resources to produce your product for the people who want to buy it? Fast-paced could also include jumping head first into a business agreement before you really understand the legalities of what you are agreeing to. Your hastiness could end up with the majority of your profit being allocated to your collaborator. The list could go on and on, but understand that every decision you make should be based on your limitations or capabilities.

3. **Find time to unplug.** Developing your business, aligning your brand and making sure that your brand identity correlates with everything that you have developed is not an easy feat. Neither is staying ahead of the competition, planning your next move, or responding to the hundreds of emails that you receive daily. I get this. Let's not take into account that you may have a family or an additional job; or perhaps even friends and hobbies.

There is a lot to do and only 23 hours to do it (you do have to factor in that one hour of sleep right?). Life is time consuming and there never seems to be enough time in the day to consume life, so how on earth are you supposed to actually stop and unplug?

In July 2014 Staples, Inc. conducted a study that found that nearly half of small business owners miss summer vacations due to a fear of unplugging. Unplugging is simply a term that represents taking a break from work to unwind and refresh. According to the survey, even when business owners take a break, two out of five people still find it hard to take their minds off of their businesses. The reasons for missed vacations varied from:

- Worrying about expenses
- Losing productivity
- Safeguarding their business assets

As a publicist, I can totally relate to this. Family and friends have often accused me of being addicted to my phone or constantly answering emails during "down time." Whether a business owner, leader, or are just a work-a-holic, it is tough to break away to relax. The truth is however, that the best way to stay productive is to find ways to break away and regroup.

Let's take baby steps. Start training to unplug by taking just 30 minutes out of your day to do something relaxing. Trust me, nothing detrimental will happen to your company in 30 minutes. Turn off the phone, tablet, computer, or whatever new digital tracking device is out there and just relax. Say it with me, "relax!" After you achieve 30 minutes without breaking into hives, try an hour and so on. I don't want you to stop working but I do want you to take the appropriate time that is necessary and required for your body to be at its best when you return to work.

There is not enough credit given to the power of relaxation. As a writer, I sometimes want to force the words to just flow. As I write this book, I can tell when my brain is on overload and it is time to let it rest for the day. Sometimes I will try to force it and when I do, it is reflective in what I've written. It sounds forced, it sounds incomplete and I always end up rewriting it the next day after

I've taken a break. Ultimately that means that I doubled the work rather than just stopping when I was tired and coming back to it after I rested. Why do we make things harder on ourselves?

I can tell you from experience that when I step away, rest my thoughts, do something totally unrelated, or just relax, it makes a world of difference when I come back to my projects. I'm sure that's the same without. It's like I mentioned about running. If a runner hasn't paced, eventually he or she will just run out of steam. You owe it to your brand, your clients, and yourself to be the best at what you do at all times. The only way that will happen is with the proper rest and recovery from all of the strenuous work that you put into your brand.

Why do you think that companies have retreats? Even with working retreats, companies orchestrate them in ways that force employees to unplug from any distractions and focus solely on the task at hand. Usually however, the objective of a retreat is to break away from all distractions and recharge so that when you return, you are ready to be even more productive. That's the same concept for unplugging.

When you unplug, you are actually doing your company a favor. You are releasing the stress and tensions that have built up and you are taking time away so that when you return, you are refreshed, energized and filled with new ideas and a new way of thinking. You may not think of a vacation or a break from the business as an investment but again, think about return; if getting away increases productivity—and it will—then that sounds like an investment worth making.

4. **Be Patient with Those Who are Being Patient with You.** I just believe that if we are going to talk about everything involved in developing your brand, then we need to talk about everything involved in developing your brand. The support and understanding of your family and friends is imperative for the journey that you have embarked on. It is extremely hard to be

productive and creative when your thoughts are consumed with how to make a friend or loved one understand why you can't do the things that you once did, or why you are always working.

As new parents to your brand, you are now adjusting to a totally new way of living. Your finances, time commitments and focus have all changed and that adjustment is not only a challenge for you; it's a challenge for your loved ones as well. I struggled with this twice: once after the birth of my child and the other after the birth of my brand. Both required tremendous time and energy and I struggled to understand why if felt as though others weren't being as understanding of my new challenges as I would have liked for them to be. Friends and family were constantly telling me that I never answer my phone, or that I am extremely hard to track down now. I even had a family member tell me that she can only find out about me by logging into social media.

I felt extremely insulted and disappointed in these people because I just didn't feel that they understood the amount of multi-tasking that I was required to do on a daily basis. I was juggling hundreds of balls in the air and just happy that nothing had fallen. In the beginning it seemed that everyone was so excited and supportive of my new ventures, but as time went on and circumstances changed, I didn't feel any real sympathy or even an attempt for them to understand what I was dealing with; and that frustrated me.

It wasn't until I had a long talk with my husband about the way I was feeling that he shared something with me that changed my entire perspective. He told me to try to be patient with him and others because they too were adjusting to the changes. He said that it would be less stressful for everyone involved if we all practiced the same patience that we wanted from the other. Isn't he just so wise!

After talking to him, it all made sense. When I really thought about it, the sudden shift in lifestyle from this new chapter in my life really was life-changing, not just for me, but for everyone connected with me. I needed to realize that my friends and family needed patience as they adjusted to the new schedules, longer hours, and infrequent communication periods just as I needed patience on my end. I was so relieved when I finally got this concept. Everyone's intentions were genuine; we just didn't realize it.

What does this have to do with you? I'll tell you. If you haven't already, you are going to have these same conversations with your loved ones and friends. You will feel pulled and tugged in every direction and when you do, just remember that it is an adjustment for everyone and once everyone becomes a little more in sync with the new life, you all will find a new normal and work well within it.

Work never ends but it does have to shift. Your priorities will shift. There are times that your business will have to take a back seat to your son's little league game, or maybe you will have to get a babysitter to pick up the kids because of an important client meeting that can't be rescheduled. The reality is that each day can call for a different priority; you have to adjust accordingly and embrace the fact that it is just not possible to be everywhere for everyone at the same time.

Now let me clarify. For me, there will never be anything more important than my family. My husband and daughter will always come first for me, but there are also times when the emphasis for the day may be my business. If I need to travel for two days for the business, that doesn't mean that my family is not still my priority, it simply means that for the next two days the emphasis is on what I need to handle for the business. This is all a part of balance. Of course I make sure that all of the arrangements and logistics to keep my house functional and everyone in place, the same way I would do for my business if my family and I decide to take a vacation. The key is to prioritize and be willing to adjust whether you work full-time and operate your business after hours, or whether your business is your full-time commitment, prioritizing and managing your time is the key to the balance that's necessary to be successful.

Work is hard; work-life balance is harder; but in the end you will figure it out. The hard part of being an entrepreneur is that there is no clock in/clock out option. There is no owner's manual for your business because you are currently writing it, so you have to stay motivated, be willing to make the necessary adjustments, of course work extra hard, and lastly rest. Don't despise the journey that you are on because there is a lesson in everything that happens in each phase of the business and brand development process. Some lessons you are learning now to implement again later down the line; some you are learning to pass along to someone else; and some are just happening to help you gain more experience in what you do.

Earlier on, I shared how my clients left their corporate jobs to pursue their dreams. This may not be your story. Your story may be completely different from theirs, but one thing that is a constant throughout the process for both of them and for you is that without the work that goes into the business, you will always end up back at the starting line. Hard work is the common denominator in every entrepreneurial story that I've ever heard or witnessed. Your audience is there, ready to buy whatever it is that you are selling, but you have to put in the work to deliver your brand in a way that makes it attractive to your customer. Whatever the case, the work has to happen and for as long as you plan to stay in business, it doesn't stop.

Chapter 11: The Power of Networking

I touched on this briefly in the earlier part of the book, but networking is so imperative to the growth of your business that I feel it's necessary to really emphasize its importance. Networking is life changing. Think about it, all it takes is a connection with the right person of influence and you can have the visibility, finances, and business partnerships that you have dreamed of. Remember in the earlier chapter when I suggested that you research the successful people who have done what you are trying to do? Well now that you know who those people are, you can find them and connect with them.

I am a part of a collective group of female entrepreneurs and every month we get together to discuss our businesses. Either through conference calls or face-to-face meetings, we get together and share our current successes, areas of improvement, and weaknesses. We encourage each other, we provide insight and ideas, and we hold each other accountable to take the necessary steps to accomplish the goals that we've shared for our businesses; and to develop our brands.

On one of our first calls, one of the ladies asked me what I would describe as a strongpoint of my business right now. I shared with her that it was my increased visibility. During that time I had experienced a major increase in the number of inquiries regarding my business and the number of meetings with potential clients. In addition, I experienced an increase in my social media followers and the number of hits that I received on my website. I was really proud of these accomplishments and so were the other ladies.

Let me take a quick moment to suggest that if you don't have a circle of trusted like-minded professionals you can confide in, you need to find a group immediately.

One of the ladies on the call asked me what factors I attributed to this increase and I, without hesitation, told her that is was totally due to networking. Networking is a valuable and necessary tool that every business owner should possess. I met my first client through networking; in fact, it was through networking that I made the decision to start my own business. Networking can move your business faster than just about any other business tactic.

A few years back, my husband and I were attending a church gala. At the gala, there was a well-known entertainer performing. Anyone who knows my husband knows that he has never met a stranger. He decided to strike up a conversation with the entertainer, which somehow led to my information being passed along because the entertainer needed a publicist. At the time, I was working full-time and only doing PR work for friends or loved ones who needed it. I did not have a formal business and I had not even actively pursued the steps necessary to start a business. What was I to do?

Later that evening my husband explained his exchange with the entertainer and told me that he would be expecting my call soon.
"Oh! I almost forgot. Give him a call; he is looking for a publicist and I told him about you," were his exact words.

Needless to say, I was thrilled and terrified at the same time.   I didn't even have business cards. This was definitely a case of putting the cart before the horse.

After interrogating my husband about what exactly he said to the entertainer, I realized that I needed to get busy pulling things together for this meeting. I needed to start taking the necessary steps to ignite my business before I called this guy. A close friend of mine guided me very quickly through the process of starting a business and was able to develop a very basic website using a customized template.   I ordered a few business cards from a local print company and jotted down the very basics of my business services so that I could at least sound knowledgeable when we spoke.

The moment of truth arrived and I met with the entertainer's manager about the possibility of working as his publicist. During that conversation, I found out that the contract was ending with their current publicist and they weren't quite sure whether they would renew it. He was pleased with my work and what I shared about my services and promised to let me know his decision by the end of the month. In the end, they decided to stick with their current publicist and I decided to continue working on my business.

And there you have it. How I got started in a nutshell all began with networking. If my husband had not just started the conversation with the entertainer, I would probably still be dreaming of "one day" starting my company. Although that client didn't work out, about three months later after I began following the steps to develop my brand, I had my first official client. And the rest, as they say, is history.

Networking. Networking. Networking. I cannot stress enough just how valuable networking is to your professional growth. It really does work. There are many people who find it extremely difficult to network because of their personalities, but I promise you it will do wonders for the advancement of your company. There are plenty of ways to work around the shyness or the insecurities of getting to know strangers, but it is definitely beneficial to your brand.

Networking is basically building relationships. If you are just starting your business and trying to penetrate a heavily saturated industry, networking helps you learn where to find your colleagues and your clients. There is a saying that I'm sure you are familiar with that says, it's not *what* you know, it's *who* you know. I believe that there is a lot of truth in that statement. If you will allow me to revise that statement a bit, I would say, "*Who* you know is just as important as *what* you know." You need both. I don't like for my clients to be the best kept secret in their industry. I think that everyone should know them and they should know everyone; that will happen quicker and more efficiently through networking.

Let me drive this point a little further. Even if you are not an entrepreneur, networking is still important. Whether you are climbing the corporate ladder or just graduating from college and entering the workforce, you need to network. It's more than attending a conference and chatting about what you do over drinks (although that's certainly not a bad thing). Networking is the process of building a bridge that will help you connect to the next point or phase in your career.

Let me just warn you that by the end of this chapter you will understand exactly why networking is so important to me. My very first job after graduating from college happened because of networking. Let's pause and recap for a moment. My first job out of college and my first client after starting my own company both happened because of networking opportunities. That's important to remember.

When I graduated college, I thought that I wanted to be a reporter. My degree was in Mass Communications: Radio/TV/Film and I had just completed my two-year internship at the local FOX affiliate in Atlanta. I had gone on several interviews for reporting and producing jobs at different TV stations in the state but just hadn't had the offer yet for the job that would catapult my broadcast career. One Sunday at church, all of the graduates for that year were honored during the service. They called each of us to the front of the church, read our names and our accolades, and then presented us with a "gift" from the congregation. After service, we all stood around receiving the many congratulations, words of encouragement, and answering the classic "do you have a job yet?" question.

Some of the graduates left the church immediately after the service, others went next door to the graduate reception, while some, like myself, decided to stick around and talk to people as long as they wanted to talk to me. After all, someone might have the broadcast journalism job that I've been waiting on. Well I was almost right. There was an older deacon who came up to me and congratulated me with a hearty handshake and asked the famous question that I mentioned earlier. I responded by letting him know that I had been on a few interviews but hadn't heard anything yet. After answering his questions about my major and skills, and the area I was looking to work in, he told me that he might have a job for me!

This gentleman named Charles Glenn, told me about a position that he knew of, and encouraged me to apply. He had connections with people in the Communications department and after a referral from him and a great interview; I was hired for my first job just two months after I graduated from college. That is what networking will do. Had I neglected to stick around and talk to others, who knows how long it would have taken to land that first job. That job introduced me to public relations and influenced my decision to focus solely on a career in PR.

There are so many benefits to networking that extend far beyond just landing a job, although that is a pretty nice benefit as well. **If nothing else, networking exposes you to other people like you or to people who need you.** Either way it is a win-win situation for you and for others. One thing is certain; networking produces opportunities. As an entrepreneur, you should always seek new opportunities and partnerships and it is so much easier to capitalize on those opportunities when you don't find yourself having to search for a contact, introduce yourself to that contact, and then convince your contact that you are the person that they need.

Let's talk for a little bit about the benefits of networking; because as I mentioned, there are plenty. Whether you are a social butterfly or an introvert, networking is a must for your business and here's why:

1. **Generates Profit**

   Well let's get right to it shall we? Networking is profitable to your business for so many reasons that I should probably write an additional book about the benefits of networking. I'll keep it simple here for now and just explain that the end result of your networking efforts will be that your business will reap positive returns. In a previous chapter, I discussed the return on investment and never has that principle applied more than when discussing networking.

Think about the story that I shared earlier about how I landed my first job through networking. I sacrificed my hunger—because after a long church service, I really wanted to go to that graduate reception and have a nice slice or two of cake— but I invested my time by staying around and talking to all of the people who came up to congratulate me on my graduation. I'm sure that I spoke to about 30 or 40 people and out of those 40 people, there was that one networking encounter that turned out to be life changing. To say life changing is no exaggeration, because not only did I profit by being connected to a job that provided a nice, steady paycheck, I also found a job that was extremely instrumental in my decision to do what I do today...16 years later. That's what I call a lasting return.

Some networking encounters may lead to another great, profitable return: clients; and businesses need clients. Less than a year ago, I was in Los Angeles with a client, fashion designer Natt Taylor. I'll talk about the networking trip in a moment. As we prepared for the trip, we knew that we would need the services of a makeup artist for an event that we were attending. My client reached out to her Atlanta makeup artist for a recommendation of someone we could use while in LA. Follow along carefully because this will all make sense in a moment.

Through this referral, we were introduced to a remarkable woman named Melissa Hibbert. Melissa is a former marketing executive turned business woman, who is the owner of her own cosmetics line, founder of the Beauty and the Business Professional Empowerment Conference, television host, and celebrity makeup artist. Yes, she wears many hats but at the time we met, she was wearing her makeup artist hat. Melissa came to our hotel and did our makeup at the recommendation of the Atlanta makeup artist. As my makeup was being applied, Melissa and I began talking. We shared with each other about our businesses and some of our upcoming projects. We ended by exchanging information and going our separate ways. That was networking. It was just a conversation between two professionals that ended in the exchange of information.

Exactly three months later, Melissa reached out to me and asked me to help her with PR efforts for an upcoming conference she was hosting in my city. I agreed and had a new client that resulted from a 20-minute encounter a few months prior. We worked together in Atlanta and the event was fantastic. A few months after that, I was back in Los Angeles as a panelist for the final stop of her conference tour. My point is that through networking, I was able to secure a new client and a new relationship while she received a service that helped her increase visibility for her project.

In addition, she had a new panelist for her conference and I had an opportunity to promote my business and gain more potential clients as a result of participating in her conference. That's profit for everyone.

To further drive my point home, I should mention that the person who initially connected us all had never met Melissa in person. They knew of each other only through social media connections and mutual industry contacts. So in the end, Melissa gained clients in us, through her networking encounters. Do you see the cycle here? Everyone in the equation gained a profit by gaining new clients, increasing visibility for their brands and building lasting relationships. That is the sole purpose and a common result of networking.

Notice that I didn't meet Melissa at a networking event, or at a conference. She was recommended by a mutual contact and we connected by simply having a conversation while she was doing her job. Imagine if neither of us said anything to each other for those 30 minutes that it took to do my makeup. That would have been a wasted opportunity to build a connection; and a profit loss for everyone involved. Networking can happen anywhere: Sharing a taxicab, waiting in line, or at a sporting event. The location is not important; anywhere you have an encounter with another person is an opportunity for you to network for your brand. It will only yield profitable returns.

2. Increases your connections.

This one is a no-brainer. The more you talk to people, the more people you know. The more people you know, the more visible you become. It really is that simple. I may have mentioned this a time or two in this book, but it bears repeating: I don't like for my clients to be the best-kept secret of anything! You will never find a client of mine with that slogan, because that means that I am not doing my job. If you are the best kept secret that means that no one knows you. If no one knows you, then how can they work with you? How can you work for them? How credible are you? The list of "hows" can go on for days.

Networking means that you are connecting with people and with each connection you are adding one more person to the list of people who know about your brand. That means there is one more person in the world who can refer your business the next time someone asks, "Hey do you know a plumber?" or "Can you recommend a good accountant?" Whatever your service is, the more people you talk to, the more people are out there who know what you do and can connect you to people who need you.

It's important to also remember that you can network with people outside of your industry. Have you ever heard of the Six Degrees of Separation theory? If not, it is the idea that six or fewer people connect everyone in the world. Everyone knows someone. There is no real proof of this theory, but it certainly seems true. Whether six, ten, or twelve degrees of separation, the concept is valid that people connect you to other people and networking is the way to find those people.

I have the perfect example: Word of Mouth. We all know that it is the best form of advertising. Word travels fast when you are really good or really bad at your service. People tell other people the good and bad news and when they do, word travels fast. Now of course we know that everyone reading this book is exceptional at what they do so why wouldn't we want people to know that. Don't underestimate the positive potential of networking with people outside of your industry. If there are only six degrees of separation, all six people will not be in your industry, but one of the six will know someone from your industry who you can connect with.

Your connections will help you get the word out about your business and in turn help generate referrals. By generating an increase in referrals through networking you are saving yourself a lot of advertising dollars. Your networks can communicate the message about your brand quicker and more efficiently than any 30-second commercial. As long as your brand is easily understood and communicated, this is a win-win situation.

3. Creates Opportunities

No one can refute the fact that anytime a group of entrepreneurs connect, there is an overwhelming sense of opportunity. What else would you expect from a group of visionaries? People who like to create are inspired when they are around other creators. Even if there are no noticeable opportunities present, people who create businesses are automatically prone to creating new opportunities to expand their businesses. They will feed off of each other's ideas and as a result, partnerships and collaborations are built and relationships are cultivated.

Just like any other parent, you and your circle of entrepreneurs should always think of ways to make your brands better. As the parent of a child, I'm always looking at new programs or activities that create great exposure for my daughter. I want each experience each day to make her a better person in some way. That should be the same motivation for everything that you do for your business.

Now here is the one caveat I must interject. Every connection is not necessarily the best connection for your brand. All potential partnerships and collaborations are not the best for your brand. **You can talk to anyone, but you cannot work with everyone.**

Before committing to any partnership, collaboration or association you should first ask yourself, "Will this make my brand better?" If the answer is yes, move forward. If the answer is no or "I'm not sure," stop and reevaluate. Everything you do from the causes that you support to your company's affiliations should be decided on by analyzing its benefit and alignment to your brand. You have birthed your brand, you understand your image and you are acting on only those things that align with your brand. Make sure to be wise in the types of ventures you become involved in. Everything you do as it pertains to your brand should still happen strategically.

Partnerships build brands. The right partnerships can elevate your business by combining the strengths of both brands. The wrong partnerships can confuse your customers and contradict your brand. When determining the potential outcome, take your time, weigh your options, evaluate the connection with your brand, and if it turns out to be a wise connection, enjoy the success of your decision.

Networking comes in several different forms. I've mentioned how networking can happen anywhere, but I should also mention the more traditional forms of networking, such as networking groups or networking activities. I told you about my collective group of female entrepreneurs; well, that group was formed because I have several friends with businesses. We are all close and one day one of the friends decided that we should be joining forces to help each other become better at what we do. That philosophy is what I consider to be a small networking group. That group is still very important in my world, and can be in yours too, because those people all know other people, and by having a better understanding of each other's businesses, we can better communicate to others about the businesses if the need presents itself. Starting groups is a great way to find out more about what is going on in your industry.

The hardest time of my life was about three months after I gave birth to my daughter Aria. My world was completely turned upside down and I didn't know which way was up. I was confused and unsure about the best way to take care of her, I didn't feel like anyone really understood where I was coming from in terms of my insecurities, and quite frankly, I was just overwhelmed. All of those books and anecdotes that I read about before she got here were out the window when she arrived. My mother and mother-in-law were great helps, but they had their own adjustments to make by being first time grandparents. My husband was adjusting to being a father, being a father to a daughter, and trying to be sensitive to his hormonal post-partum wife! Poor man!

Because of this, everyone involved had a hard time figuring out the other person's perspective and we all just felt our way through by taking it day by day. As the mother; however, I needed more. I needed someone who understood exactly what I was going through and I needed answers. So I formed my own group of new moms who all had children between newborn and one year old. This network of moms was vital, I believe, to our transition into motherhood. We met monthly, talked daily and shared our feelings, experiences, challenges, triumphs, remedies and anything else that came up on this new journey. The network of moms continues four years later. Some have additional children, while others of us still have one child but the concept of our original startup was the same. We wanted to be better and we were there to help each other achieve that goal.

The same can and should happen with you and your brand through networking. It's not always about the profit or the potential industry advancement that can happen through networking; networking can be just as beneficial to your growth and knowledge of your industry as it can to your profit margin. Just as I did with my network of women entrepreneurs and my network of moms, you can join or form your own networking groups of like-minded entrepreneurs who can help you grow through advice and mentorship. You in return can do the same for them.

There are organizations that specifically host networking events for their industry. It's a productive way to learn from others, stay informed of the trends in the industry and access people that may be hard to reach in any other setting. The great thing about these networks is that no one has to be the expert and everyone has something to contribute.

If you are uncomfortable with attending meetings, or operating in a face-to-face setting, start small with social networking. I know an entrepreneur with a brand that is growing daily by leaps and bounds. On social media he has more than 30 thousand followers and has a waiting list for clients. He has perfected his social media campaign to the point that he may need to write his own book about social networking. He posts videos, hosts chats, and seminars, and has clients figuratively knocking down his door for his service. The amazing thing to me is how shy he is in person. He is extremely kind but has admitted that his strength lies at his fingertips behind the computer. To see his social media campaign, you would never think that he was as shy as he is.

A self-described introvert in person, he obviously recognizes the importance of networking so he found a way to thrive despite his insecurities. Let me clarify; social networking is not his only form of networking but it is what's most comfortable. He still has meetings and communicates with people, but he has found a way to capitalize on his strengths to make up for the areas that are lacking. I recommend this strategy for anyone who is learning to network more. The key is to do it in whatever way you can. Traditional networking will become more comfortable as time continues but this is a great way to get started.

If you need to, start out by just attending conferences and networking events. After you get there and have been in the atmosphere a few times you can work on building the courage to just speak to people; but at least you are in the room with your colleagues. The next step is to find at least two people that you can strike up a conversation with and exchange information. Perhaps it is the person sitting next to you at the table or the person standing behind you in the drink line; where you start the conversation doesn't matter as long as you start it. The last recommendation is to build on the conversations that people start with you. Believe it or not, people see you as someone worth getting to know as well. They want to connect with you just as much as you want to connect with others. If someone tries to strike up a conversation with you at these events, don't make it difficult for them. Talk back!

I attended an event with a friend of mine because she needed a plus one. She warned me that she doesn't like talking to people and would probably leave after the program ended. Did she actually think that she would skip out on the networking portion with me, the PR girl, as her date? Like clockwork, after the main program ended she was ready to leave. I wouldn't let her. We stood around for a bit and finally I challenged her to just talk to someone. She declined and the next thing I knew we were headed to the coat check to get our belongings. The line was backed up and we found ourselves waiting for an extended period of time with a few others. The lady standing in front of my friend turned around and said to her, "I'm glad that I'm not in a hurry." My friend just smiled at her.

As we continued to stand, the lady turned around again and said, "Do you all have an early day in the morning?" My friend said, "No." Well this was not only awkward; it was a bit ridiculous. The lady was trying to network with us, but my dear, sweet friend left her helpless with those close-ended answers. Being the super plus one that I am, I decided to take over and continue the conversation and eventually my friend joined in. They later found out that both worked at different times at the same company and exchanged cards. That, my friends, was networking. I don't know if they ever touched base or utilized each other's services but one thing was for sure, had my friend continued to make it difficult for the lady to talk to her, nothing would have resulted from all that time standing in that coat check line.

I think that this would be a good point to assign homework. Whether networking comes easily or not, or whether you prefer social media networks or face-to-face interactions, I would like to challenge you to either join or attend a networking event in some capacity. Research upcoming events for your industry in your city, and just visit to see who is there. If that's too big of a step for you then I challenge you to reach out via social media on

Linked In, Facebook, Twitter, or Instagram and find people who do what you do. Once you find them, connect with them. Post on their page, reply to a comment that they've posted, or inbox them directly with a request to connect further. Whatever is the most comfortable method for you, do it. After you do, do it again, and again, and again. Before you know it, it will become second nature and you will be a lean, mean, networking machine.

Chapter 12: **It's Time to Connect**

O nce upon a time not long ago in fact, there was an unwritten rule (actually someone probably did write it down) that if a business did not have a website, it was not a valid business. No matter how large or small the business or product; you needed an online presence. Whether you had a product that had the potential for online retail or not, your business needed a website so that your audience, potential clients, potential collaborators, or anyone else could find out more information about you and the company.

I attended a networking event back in the early 2000s. It was designed for young professionals who were looking to connect with other young professionals. The event was a meet and greet mixer where young professionals met at a different location monthly and networked. It was a fun, social event but also a great opportunity to meet new people. While I was there I met a photographer and we began discussing our work. He gave a great elevator speech about his work and business. He was a freelancer and was always looking to work with companies and organizations that hosted events and needed a photographer to capture the moments.

In my opinion, this guy really could have quit his photography gig to travel the world giving lectures on how to pitch your company to potential clients. He was great and I was sold. I was working in PR for a health system at the time and we hosted quite a few fundraisers along with community and social events. We had an in-house photographer, but we occasionally used freelancers as well. I was really impressed with this gentleman and wanted to pass his information along to the appropriate people back at work so I asked him for a card. He obliged and as I looked it over, I noticed that there was no website address.

I asked him if he could just tell me the name of his site and you won't believe what he told me: "I don't have a website." "What?" I thought. This guy just gave the best company pitch that I'd ever heard in my short time of hearing company pitches and I was ready to pass his information along, but he did not have a website. At that very moment he dropped from the professional photographer category to the "photography is my hobby" category. How could he not have a website? If he had written down the spiel that he gave me, he would have had all the content he needed for a site. Unfortunately, I never passed along his information and we never crossed paths again.

Although I am sure by now that photographer has a website and probably several social media accounts, and he is probably doing very well for himself; at that time I just couldn't view him as an experienced professional without any way of looking at his background, work samples, company information, and history online. I certainly didn't feel comfortable referring him to my "powers that be" simply based on what he told me. He was not credible to me because he did not have a website and as harsh as that may seem, many of you have probably felt the same way about a company as well.

That encounter happened during a time when the idea that every business needed a website was just starting to become popular. Some companies embraced the idea while others resisted it and viewed it as a necessity only for certain types of companies. If you were a web developer or designer, or you had a product that you could sell in an online store, a website was a given necessity. Others who were less pressed to develop their own site analyzed their needs a little differently. The fact remained that back then *everyone* big, small or in between, needed a website and that is still a fact today.

We talked about your website site earlier, but I just want to make a few correlations to your website and social media. The first is that both are part of your brand identity. Just like the logo and your company name, everything must align. The photos that you use, the messages that you communicate, the videos or blogs or any other type of communication that you incorporate into your website should all align with the brand that you have so carefully developed. We talked earlier about the different responsibilities of social media accounts and your website. One was that social media is the resume that drives your potential clients to your website (the interview) and there they determine whether or not you get the job. Let's discuss this job interview for a moment because there certain visual particulars that you must be aware of before you step foot in the interview and those also apply to your website. These particulars include:

1. Professional attire
2. A clean, well-polished appearance
3. A solid, carefully crafted resume
4. A clear, concise message that you can communicate about why your service is needed

Those principles match perfectly for this scenario because the goal of both a job interview and a visit to your website is the same: to get the job!

Professional Attire: Your appearance is the very first thing that your potential employer notices on a job interview. Before you open your mouth to speak, the interviewer is approaching you and can see everything about you from head to toe. Are you professionally dressed? Do you have on the proper hosiery? Are your shoes appropriate? Are you wearing a jacket and tie? The answers to those questions are important because our society has a standard or style guide for how to dress for an interview. If you are not compliant with those standards, then you already have strikes against you.

This is the same philosophy for your website. Your website's professional attire is basically its professional look and alignment to your brand. When your potential client or partner visits your site, what they see can leave a lasting impression. The opinions immediately begin to form and the alignment of your brand helps to mold those opinions towards your original intent.

The problems begin when your website does not visually align with your brand. For instance, if part of your brand is that you are calm, relaxed and level-headed, then your website should reflect that. You should not have the bold colors and flashy images that indicate the exact opposite of your brand. This sends mixed signals about your business. Your website should be consistent with who you are as a company. Across the board with all of the marketing materials and deliverables, your site should look the part.

A Clean Well-Polished Appearance

What I mean by clean, well-polished site is that your site needs to make sense. It is so frustrating and even overwhelming to visit a website and find everything on the home page. I mean everything. I'm sure you have seen websites where the home page is cluttered with pictures, colors and content, and there is no true organization about the information that is presented. That's not what I mean by polished.

When you are on a job interview, your shirt is tucked in, your shoes are tied, your hair is neat, your clothes are ironed, some of you may even shine your shoes; and all of that can be described as clean and polished. Heading to a job interview while looking as though you just finished a great workout, or as if you just rolled out of bed, even while wearing professional attire, probably won't leave the best impression with the potential client.

Unfortunately we live in a vain society where people judge you and the quality of your work or your personality based on how you look. This goes for your website as well. When developing your site, make sure that it is clean by ensuring the following.

- Your navigation bar is visible
- You have enough white space on the page
- There aren't a lot of busy colors and pictures

This sounds like a pretty simple task but it actually can become difficult because our first instinct, when developing our sites, is to include everything on the home page so that no one misses anything. If the navigation bar is visible and pretty straightforward like a roadmap, then there won't be any need to crowd everything on the home page because visitors will understand where everything is located.

An aesthetically pleasing website speaks volumes about your brand. It shows that you took your time to align the site with your brand, core values and overall key messages. The white space that I mentioned simply means just that, the more white space on your web page, the neater and easier to read it will be. The viewer's eyes are directed to a particular focal point and not scrambling to filter through a lot of clutter in order to figure out what to read.

Quite frankly when I view messy, busy, or cluttered websites, I don't stick around very long to find what I'm looking for. I imagine that most web viewers operate the same way. Excessive photos that replace text, or elaborate fonts that are hard to read make it really difficult to find the key message of the site. After all, people come to your website to find out more in-depth information about you and your business. They don't want to just look at pictures; they would like a visually appealing road map that leads to pertinent content and information that will help them determine if you are the right person for the job.

A Solid, Carefully Crafted Resume

This is probably my favorite point of this chapter. As I've stated before, the resume is what gets you the job interview, not the job. Truthfully, the average employer spends less than a few minutes scanning your resume for relevant information. After the quick scan—or review of your resume-- an employer then decides if he or she would like to take the time to get to know more about you and explore the potential of hiring you for the job. A resume should stand out; it should list your qualifications, experiences, work history, contact information, and any other relevant information that will help the hiring manager determine if you are worth getting to know further.

For all practical purposes let's think of the components of your website as your resume. Your viewers are only going to spend a few minutes scrolling through your pages, clicking on a few navigation tabs, and actually reading the content that you have provided before they make that final decision to either learn more or move on. Your website has to stand out; in fact, I think that by this point of the book you have realized that whatever it is that you do, you must stand out when doing it.

Here are a couple of ideas to remember about your site to help increase the chances of your viewers sticking around to learn more.

1. **Your website content must align perfectly with your brand.** Other than you, your website is probably the most tangible representation of your brand that your audience will find. **Don't be unrecognizable to your clients when they visit your website.** Your site is your mouthpiece, your image and your personality all right at the fingertips of your viewer. Since this is the case, it's imperative that your brand is accurately

represented on your site. The look, verbiage, and messages should reflect all of the ideas that we developed about your brand in the earlier chapters.

Remember that repetition is key to the communication and understanding of your brand. Clients cannot hear one thing about your brand and see a totally different representation on your website. By now you should have a style guide for your brand. (If not, simply filter through all of the notes that you've taken throughout this book and develop one...if you've followed along, all of the content is there) Your style guide is your branding manual or protocol for everything pertaining to your brand and brand image from the font name and size of your logo to the core values and key messages. All of the components of your branding style guide should be reflected on your website. Think of it this way, your website should be a clone of your vision for your brand. What do your clients see when they visit your site?

2. **All relevant information should be easily accessible.** I will keep this simple. Everything

that people need to know about you should be easy to find on your website. Here's a checklist to make sure that you are covering all of the key areas that viewers seek when searching your site:

- Home page – Aside from being visually appealing, it should contain just enough information to make the viewer want to know more.

- About Us/History - Everyone needs a little history lesson. This tab will help the client learn more about your business, such as why and how you started, how you have grown, and where you are currently.

- Services/Rates - This tab lets clients know what type of services you provide and your rates for service. Not all websites include the exact rate because it may depend on varying factors, but there should at least be information about how to receive a quote or additional information.

- Clients - People like to know who else has utilized your services. If you can provide client testimonials, this is helpful as well. A small list of past clients is nice but definitely not necessary, especially if your business has not grown to that point.

- Gallery - A video or photo gallery of your venue, product, service, events, etc., is helpful for your potential clients. The key is to make sure to use high quality photos and videos.

- Contact - How can they follow up with you if you have no contact information? Make sure that clients know how to find you via phone, email, speaking engagements, and social media networks.

There may be more information for you to add to your site or there may be less as it pertains specifically to your brand. The main objective here is for you to figure out exactly what your clients need to know to help them decide whether or not they will utilize your service. Think about the things that you look for when you visit other websites or businesses. Most importantly, think about what information you can provide that will help you secure the job.

Today, over a decade later, the same philosophies that I just mentioned apply for not only websites, but also for social media. The difference between websites and social media is that after a website is developed, the process for updating, revising content, etc., becomes routine. With social media however, the challenge becomes that as soon as you master one network, gain a decent number of followers/friends, and really find your rhythm with posting and responding, an entirely new type of social media network pops up starting the whole learning process over again.

Social media has grown into its own unique animal and I get that it can be extremely frustrating and time consuming, but believe me when I tell you that you have to jump on this bandwagon. Today the perception of social media has turned into what the perception of websites once was. If you don't have a social media account as a business, you may not be considered valid or credible. There are so many benefits to social media:

1. You are able to connect daily with your audience
2. You are able to gain instant feedback from your audience

3. You are able to increase your visibility quicker and find new contacts instantly

Connecting with your audience. Any opportunity to connect with your audience is a great opportunity. Social media is more than posting a few pictures or gaining a few "likes" for a cool comment. Social media is a communication method that keeps you constantly on your audience's radar. Through social media you become more accessible, your audience becomes more accessible, and you begin having daily conversations with one another. What's the most important aspect of a relationship? Communication. Your relationship with your audience strengthens through social media because of the constant communication that you share.

Insta-Feedback. Before Twitter, Instagram, Facebook, Snapchat, or Periscope, companies had letters, emails, and phone calls to help them learn the opinions of their clients. Nowadays the idea of feedback is both a blessing and a curse. Companies look to social media to find out what their audience is thinking. And now audiences take to social media to voice their opinions whether good or bad.

Recently I was watching a reality competition on television. The host of the show was interviewing one of the contestants and used the word "amazing" profusely. I noticed the word use as I watched, but never in a million years did I think of taking that to social media. After the commercial break the host mentioned to other cast members that she was going to stop saying the word because social media posts indicated that there was a drinking game going on and every time she said amazing, someone would have to take a drink.

That feedback was discovered almost instantly through social media. In a matter of two minutes, the network was able to find out what their audience thought of the show. If you've noticed, there are now social media feeds at the bottom of live shows that display some of the posts and opinions of the viewers. Now if word can travel that fast, it is important to stay on top of social media efforts so that your company and brand can adjust accordingly to the fast-pace spread of opinions about your brand.

Increased Visibility. It's almost impossible to forget a person you see and hear of every day. Every post, tweet, or video that you send has the potential to become profitable. A simple repost, or retweet has the potential to gain you a dozen or more followers just by the endorsement of another person. Think of social media as an instant referral. When a user sees a repost from their "friend," most times they will check out the person or company that originally posted just to see what else that company has said or done.

If your company has a sale or special, social media can spread the word just as quickly as any other form of advertising. A great way to increase your visibility is to follow others in your industry who have an aggressive social media campaign. Chat with them, repost their comments and help each other push your agendas to your potential clients.

I should probably back up a bit and make sure that you know a few social media terms. A post is a comment or status that you leave on your page. It could be a photo, video, or words that describe how you are feeling, what you are doing, or an opinion about current events, or industry-related topics. Your page is a blank canvas to be painted however you choose. A repost, or in the case of Twitter, a retweet, is the process of sharing someone else's post that you agree with. For instance, if I posted "Today is first day of the rest of your life," you may decide that you like that and also want to share it with your followers, so you repost it. Depending on the social media site, the terminology may be different but the concept is the same.

Regardless of which site you are visiting, you should still be interactive. It's a great idea to figure out the best time of day and frequency of posting that works for you. I have a client who posts first thing in the morning. This is because her audience consists of working adult women. These are women who wake up early and check their social media sites before starting their workday. She posts again later in the day because that will cover the time zone difference. If she is on the East Coast and posts at nine in the morning, then it may be too early for her peak audience. Posting later in the day allows her to reach audiences on both sides of the country at different times.

If you are wondering how to figure out your best times for posting, simply observe your audience. I did this and discovered that either early morning posts or after work posts garner the best results for me. I aim to reach people before and after the typical workday. I do this because during the time that I was posting several times a day, I found that certain times yielded no likes or comments while other times almost instantly garnered likes, comments, and in some cases new followers.

You can also figure out your most productive posting times by doing the same thing. Notice when you get the most followers, likes, or comments and rather than wasting time posting when no one is watching, maximize your time by posting when necessary. Watch how quickly you will gain more followers and learn more about them. Communication is the key to connecting with your audience.

Please allow me to touch on a tricky but important social media topic for just a moment. Social media is great for your business; we know that, but it's also great for your personal life in that the same way it helps you connect with your clients, it helps you stay connected to your family and friends. My husband and I have family in various parts of the country as do most people. Our social media usage boosted significantly after our

244 CONGRATULATIONS! IT'S A BRAND.

daughter was born, because we wanted to share all of her funny moments, infamous stories and conversations and of course random pictures with our families and friends who did not have a chance to see her daily. We live almost an hour away from both sets of her grandparents, so her daily school outfit postings and other videos are great to post on social media so that everyone can see what she is up to.

We also post about our ventures and funny moments, etc. It's such a great tool for staying connected to family and friends that you just wouldn't otherwise communicate with so frequently. The problem can occur when your business and personal pages mesh on social media. What do I mean? I mean that the brand becomes confusing when viewers view family photos, or even more personal posts on a social media page that is supposed to represent your business.

I know; I know you are saying in your head, "Celebrities do this all the time," and this is true but the difference is:

1. They are celebrities; and there really are no rules for celebs.

2. Celebrities have a personal brand that includes the entire scope of their lives.

Personal brands and social media are different than corporate or traditional business brands and social media. It may be appropriate to share more personal aspects of your life when developing your personal brand. When you have a traditional brand; however, the personal aspects, such as family vacations, the family pet, and the infamous bathroom selfie are not as appropriate.

Most entrepreneurs have both a personal and a business brand. In this case the accounts should be separate. I have clients who are two completely different people on social media, literally. They manage both their business and personal accounts, but the content is completely separate. This is important to remember, because it all boils down to your brand. Personal photos and videos on your business page, whether incriminating or not, do not help your brand. The great thing about social media is that it reaches an enormous amount of people in a short amount of time. The bad thing about social media is pretty much the same. The wrong post or the wrong message also reaches that enormous amount of people in a short amount of time. A good rule to follow when thinking of what do concerning your brand is this, "if it's not helping it, it's hurting it." Be careful not to mix messages on social media.

In a nutshell, social media is extremely important to your brand's visibility. With the constant changes, new apps, updates, web resources, and trends, it's important to create and build your social media presence now so that you aren't too far behind tomorrow. As daunting as it is to keep up, the key is to start with one outlet, find your rhythm, gain your following, and use that momentum as leverage for the next social media outlet that you choose. Remember, your social media networks should not replace your website, it should help you drive clients to your website. As long as your posts are consistent with your brand, social media interaction will help you catapult that brand's visibility in an instant.

Chapter 13: **Your Brand is Valuable**

I f you haven't guessed by now, I'm a writer. I strongly believe in the power of words and I really believe in the power of written words. There is a difference between verbal and written communication, especially when it pertains to how you communicate to yourself. This may sound a little strange but I think that rather than talking to yourself, which is what many of us do whether we would like to admit it or not; we should write to ourselves. Yes, you heard me. I think that a different level of productivity happens when we write things down. I've talked about that a lot throughout this book because it's true. In this chapter, I am going to show you how writing can actually increase your business profit.

If you think about it, the concept of writing to yourself is really not that hard to understand. Most kids, especially young girls, have diaries and boys—although it's the same concept—may refer to it more as journaling.

Journaling has become increasingly popular as of late and most people who journal actually say that it is therapeutic.

There was a blog in the April 15, 2015 edition of The Huffington Post that shared the benefits of keeping a journal. The blog mentioned benefits such as stretching your IQ, evoking mindfulness, achieving goals, increasing intelligence, boosting memory and a few others. I agree wholeheartedly with each of their findings, especially the point about achieving goals. During your conception and pregnancy stages, we talked about how achieving goals is directly related to writing down your goals; and of course, answering them. I want to share one more benefit that writing provides to your business. It helps you increase your income by realizing your value.

Writing is essentially the transfer of thoughts to paper. It turns those ideas and thoughts that are in your head into tangible actions by seeing them on a piece of paper. Just as it's a necessity for you to write down your goals and all of the other aspects that we've established thus far, it is equally as important to write down what you have accomplished. The next best reason to write things down, other than to see where you are headed is so that you can assess where you currently are in your business.

Sometimes as we go through the hustle and bustle of our daily lives, we may not necessarily realize how many things we are able to accomplish in a day. Think about it; if you were to write down every single task that you completed throughout the day—large or small—you are sure to be amazed at all that was accomplished.

Trust me, if you write down everything that you did in a day from the moment you woke up to the moment that you lay back down for the night, you would probably have quite a few items on that list. Now imagine if you did that for the week, or for the year, or for a career span. It would almost be as if you were daily tracking items for your resume. There are certain things that you do throughout the day that are just second nature and you don't really view them as time consuming or a challenge, or something that may be difficult for someone else to achieve. You just go throughout your day or your career doing what you do and moving on to the next thing.

Let me explain where I am going with this. When you write down everything that you do, you realize that you are worth a lot more than you may realize. What I mean by that is you can see everything that you are able to accomplish and you may actually be surprised. Let me give you an example. Let's pretend the following is your typical day:

- Wake up
- Restroom
- Shower
- Get dressed
- Wake up the kids
- Pick out their clothes
- Dress the kids
- Groom the kids (i.e. comb hair, brush teeth, etc.)
- Prepare breakfast
- Pack everyone up to leave the house
- Secure everyone in the car
- Drive to school
- Drop off kids
- Drive to work

This is just a very general list and there are already 14 items on the list. There could actually be more or less items on this list, depending on quite a few specific circumstances, but for the sake of the example you have already completed 14 tasks within the first hour or two of your day. That's quite an accomplishment. I'll just estimate that on the low end, by the end of the day, you have accomplished nearly 100 items on this list. Let's not forget that your list will probably triple once you start your work day and then it will grow again when you head into the evening activities. Whew!

Now imagine if someone asked you to perform a really big task on this day that we've just outlined. Without realizing what you have on your plate for the day, you may hastily agree to do what was asked. If you were aware of every responsibility for the day, then you may be better able to realistically determine whether you can fulfill the request or not. A huge problem with people overextending themselves is that they don't realize everything that is already on their plates when they make extra commitments. They underestimate their responsibilities and overextend their generosity; as a result stress, chaos, and panic probably enter the equation at some point. Hang with me because I really am going somewhere with this.

Underestimating yourself often results in undervaluing your worth and underestimating comes from not realizing all that you have accomplished. This pertains to life and business but we will stick with the purpose of this book and focus on business. When I refer to your value, I am referencing both your time and your rate. One of the hardest decisions to make as a business is determining what you will charge for your service. We all struggle with it because there is no true algorithm that will give you the answer to your true value. Let's face it both time and money are two important facets of your business. Do you have time to do it and do you have the money to do it? The struggle with determining how to make the time and the money is every entrepreneur's headache.

I recommend writing down your accomplishments because it provides tangible evidence to you and your clients of what you have accomplished. It validates why you require what you do to do what you do. Now I gave the example of writing down everything that you do in a day just to help you realize that even in your personal time, you accomplish more than you realize. In the list above if that were your day and you hadn't written down those 14 completed tasks, you may have only remembered waking up, feeding the kids, taking them to school, and going to work. That's four out of the 14 things that you actually did. That same principle applies to the way you record your business achievements.

When you finally realize that all of your education, achievements, experience, and clients actually amount to your credibility as a business professional, you will have no problem charging your rate or accepting or denying the clients or business of your choosing. Why? Because you know what you are worth. Take the time to really update your resume, not to pass out to a potential employer, but for your own personal record of what makes you qualified to do what you do. You will be surprised and impressed and you will think better of the work that you do along with the rate that you charge.

When I had my daughter, I went through a time when I was extremely overwhelmed because just as the new parent of a business, when you have a child your life is completely thrown off. There are a lot of adjustments. It becomes overwhelming because you have to figure out how you will adapt to this new way of living because it is not a temporary situation. For the next 18 years plus, you will have that child under your roof and for the next 18 years plus, you will have that business in some capacity. So it was an adjustment for me. I tried to accomplish all of the tasks that I had before the child and still incorporate her into my new way of living. I had no clue about all that I had committed myself to and as a result, I made everything harder on myself. If I had taken the time, which I later did, to analyze all that I was responsible for, I would have been able to figure out better strategies for parenting, working, being a spouse, and living. That's all I'm trying to get you to do.

Don't make work harder on yourself by not realizing your value. If you perform a service and there is only one of you performing that service, then you may need to increase your prices so that you can hire someone to share the load. Otherwise you will find yourself underpaid, overworked, and less productive. The goal of being an entrepreneur is not to make things harder on you. You want to figure out ways to give your clients superb customer service without stressing yourself out.

I'll just go ahead and talk about it; it is difficult, financially, to be the owner of a business. You are solely responsible for your income and perhaps the income of others. You don't have the same types of securities as someone who has a steady paycheck at a traditional job, so every decision that you make must be a wise one. That's a huge challenge, but in order to complete the goal, you must know your true value and be confident about it.

Here are some tips to help you realize your true worth:

1. **Compensation is vital to survival.** Let's face it. Yes, you started your business because you have a passion for what you do, but quite frankly you also intend to be compensated well for your work. That being said, I do realize that there are times during your entrepreneurial journey where you may have to provide work solely for the experience and exposure. The value of being in a certain environment or working with a particular client may be worth more and have more long-term effects than that of a short-term dollar amount. I am totally in support of utilizing the barter system where you may exchange beneficial

products and services in exchange for experience, exposure, or connections. As you grow; however, you will need to be more selective about when you forgo a paycheck for a connection or experience.

Let me give you an example. Not long ago, I had a consultation with a client about whether or not a potential business collaboration was beneficial. He wanted advice on whether or not he should provide a potential client with samples of his product. He followed up by sharing with me that he receives requests for samples or free products quite often in exchange for publicity. The requestor is usually well known or connected to someone who is well known and will advertise on their social media sites about my client's product. At the time of our conversation, he wanted my opinion on whether or not he should grant the request to donate his product in exchange for advertisement.

I advised my client against moving forward with the offer. I shared with him that at this point in his career he could be more selective about his affiliations. The person requesting his service was not extremely well known and only needed the product for a particular event. If he provided the product at no cost then he would ultimately be giving away his product with no return. The only advertisement would be via social media and although the requestor had a decent amount of followers, not all of those followers even encompassed his audience. There would be no profitable return on that investment.

Now what I also advised him to do is what I just mentioned to you. I told him to write down all that he has accomplished within the last two years and assess how far his business has grown from the first year to current. He later came back to me and shared that he had not even realized that he had progressed from being a novice to an accomplished professional within the last three years of his career. Prior to analyzing his credentials, he still saw himself as the entrepreneur who just needed someone to believe in him. He has steady clients now; an established brand, and is headed into a larger platform to promote his product. He is starting to realize his worth.

2. **Go ahead and raise your prices.** I don't know you; I'll admit that, but one thing that I do know is that you are not charging enough. How do I know? I know because I have those same struggles; my colleagues have those struggles and probably every entrepreneur has the "am I charging too much" struggle at some point in their career. It's tough, I understand. You want to get paid, you want to have customers, and you don't want to run anyone away.

At the beginning of your journey, you probably had a price that you were comfortable with until it was time to provide the customer with the quote. Then you began to second guess yourself and ask, "Is this too much? Are they really going to pay this much? Am I overcharging?"

I remember a time at the very beginning of my entrepreneurial experience when I was faced with giving my potential client my fees. I gave a great sell of the business and services, felt really good about the potential of the new relationship, and knew that the final decision would be based on the rate that I provided. Now I already knew that my rates for this project were considerably lower than my competitors (which is a huge no-no) but I still was nervous about what I would charge. I sent my potential client the quote and immediately called to "confirm" that she received it. The conversation went this way.

"Hi X, I was just following up to confirm that you received the quote," I said.

"Yes, it just popped up so I will take a look and let you know my decision soon," he said.

"OK, great. If you have any questions about anything just let me know; and if the quote is out of your budget we can talk about a discount; it's not a problem."

What in the world was I thinking!!! I was already discounting what was already too low before he even saw the original quote. I wanted the business so bad that I guess I would have done if for next to free. Guess what happened? The client called me and immediately asked about the discount, of course. At that point I had to oblige and the next three months of our contract, I worked way harder than what I was being paid to do. In fact, thinking back on it, I probably lost out on other clients because I was doing so much work that I couldn't take on anyone else. Now that would have been perfectly fine if I had charged enough to compensate me and any other business that I may have lost as a result of the work that I needed to do.

Am I saying that I should have charged him the equivalent of three clients? Yes!! If that was what the work would have added up to. In any industry, bigger projects or bigger demands require a larger rate.

If the plumber is coming to your home to fix the leaky sink in your bedroom, they will charge you a certain rate; but if you decide that you need the guest bathroom sink fixed, then the bill total increases. If you go to a salon and just get a simple style, that's one price, but if after you get there you decide that you want a trim and maybe a few highlights, that's a huge increase—trust me, I know from experience! You are just as worthy to be paid for your services as the next person. Look at your competitors' prices, if you have the same type of clientele, same type of experience and services, then you should probably be closer to their price or even higher depending on your brand.

I am in no way promoting price gouging but I do want you to understand that you are in business to make a profit. Otherwise you would be doing what you do as a hobby. Your brand also dictates your prices. I know that if I stay at certain hotels; I will pay more per night than at others. The quality of your work should match the price but even if part of your brand is that you are affordable, you should still be affordable within reason. Look at what it will cost you to do the job, add in your experience and credentials, add in other factors, such as the amount of time that it will take to either perform the service or deliver the product, couple that with what the industry standard is and be confident in your rate and stick to it!

3. **Be selective with your customer.** Let me say from the beginning that I am *not* condoning discrimination here. What I am saying is that it is fine to turn down work. If you find that a customer can't utilize your service due to your rates, then that's not your customer. There are people out there who will pay for your service. Look at it this way; perhaps you have come to a crossroads in your business where your clientele is changing. Believe me, there are people out there who will pay for your service, so don't chase after the ones who say that they won't.

I helped to plan a party not too long ago for a friend and I was in charge of finding the caterer. Now this was to be a simple get together that was very casual and not a lot of pomp and circumstance. I wanted to find a caterer to provide light hors d'oeuvres for the occasion. There were certain caterers that I didn't even bother reaching out to for this event because I knew that their rates would not be within the budget for this particular party.

As I continued to search and seek caterers, I talked to many; they provided quotes, but some were a little too costly for what we were trying to do and others were not. The ones that were too costly stood by their rates. They informed me that because of travel, delivery, the food presentation, the type of food that I wanted, and other factors, they had to charge what they charged and they made no attempts to discount the price. I respected that and politely shared that I would not be able to utilize their services. They politely said they understood and let me go.

That's what you do in business; you stay true to your brand, its reputation and your prices. I wasn't their customer for that particular event, but please understand that both the representative and I knew that just as I declined their work, someone else would call and accept it. That's what I mean when I say that you must understand your value. You can't secure every customer, but you can work hard to find the customer who will accept your rates and appreciate your work.

As I end, I just want to reemphasize that I understand that this part of the business is a challenge because everyone wants customers. We all want to be the preferred resource for our industry. That's a very realistic goal, by the way but also understand that the respect from your industry comes with you first respecting yourself. Don't belittle your own value by chasing opportunities that are not the most beneficial for your growth in the first place. Companies prove all the time that you can have the rates that you require and still secure the audience that will support that. I am personally more confident with my rates now than I ever have been and that comfort level for you will continue to grow as your business grows. In the meantime reassess your value and make sure that the way you portray your brand in pricing, opportunities, and clientele lives up to the brand that you have defined. It all comes back to branding.

Chapter 14: The PR Talk

Some readers may be surprised that I chose to dedicate only one chapter specifically to public relations; but truthfully, this entire book is about PR. The strategies that we've discussed, the questions that we've pondered thus far are all tactics and areas that are emphasized through public relations. This book really does capture the idea of the job of a public relations professional. We help you think about your brand in a way that will create longevity, success, and increased visibility. With answers or at least an idea of everything that we have discussed, you are now in a position to implement some PR strategies to increase the visibility of your brand.

We've talked about blurred lines before in this book, but never has the line been more blurred than when it comes to the topic of marketing, advertising and public relations. In theory I can understand why it may seem that these three concepts are the same or quite similar; but there are noticeable differences between the two that as an entrepreneur you need to know. Before I begin a consultation with clients, I let them know a few things up front. Usually it begins with a definition of public relations. **PR is the effort based on strategy to increase visibility through non-paid publicity.**

Non-paid publicity is what distinguishes PR from advertising. It is what we call in the business "earned media" and basically, it means that you are not paying for coverage of your brand. Commercials, magazine ads and radio spots are all considered paid advertisements. With PR, on the other hand, the interviews that you hear on the radio and the articles that you read in the newspaper or magazines are non-paid. A publicist has developed a relationship with those outlets, used PR tools, such as pitching and relationship building and secured those opportunities for their clients. There is an entire philosophy around how to make those things happen that I won't get into, because that's a different type of book, but with the right publicist or THE WRITE MEDIA GROUP (shameless plug), your brand's audience will benefit from PR.

I'm not just saying this because I'm a publicist, but public relations has far more lasting effects than advertising. The first is that PR doesn't cost. Let me be clear, it does cost to hire a PR professional, but it does not cost for a journalist to report about your brand. Think of it this way, a full-page, color ad in a reasonably popular magazine could cost you on the low end around five to seven thousand dollars. This is a very generic example based on the lower end fee range, of a non-mainstream, reasonably popular magazine. For that amount of money, that full-page ad appears in one issue of the magazine. It does not guarantee the online component either. Meanwhile the same information that was placed in an ad could be covered on a popular news, talk, or radio show, or a magazine at no cost. Not only that, but a link to the show will be archived and can be repurposed for your and the media outlet's future use.

Another difference between public relations and advertising is that through PR, your audience has an opportunity to hear from you directly. They have a chance to see you, hear your story more in depth and learn more about you through interviews, speaking engagements, collaborations, events, and articles. Paid advertising is usually very short and concise. The audience doesn't have a chance to learn much from a 20 second commercial that is usually done in someone else's voice. An interview is more intimate. Even though some interviews are shorter than others, they still give your audience an opportunity to see you or your product and engage with you even for a brief encounter.

A couple of years ago, Fox's American Idol winner Fantasia Barrino appeared as a guest on a popular daytime talk show. I happened to be home at that time and I tuned in because she was going to share a lot about her journey since her American Idol win. She had gone through a few challenges at the time that were very high profile and in this interview, which was the first since her negative publicity, she was going to share her story in her words, as well as promote her new album. Prior to this interview, I was not a huge Fantasia fan, although I did and still do love her voice, so stumbling upon her interview was pure coincidence. I listened to her story and the very candid answers to some tough questions by the show's host. I was impressed and I was moved. I was so moved, in fact, that I immediately downloaded her new album right after the interview. I don't know that a mere "buy Fantasia's new album" commercial would have had that same effect.

Public relations is about a relationship between you and everyone that concerns you. Your public is getting to know you (or your product). It's about finding ways to connect and stay connected to your audience so that you are engaged with each other. Your reach is far wider with PR than it is with advertising because again, the outlet that you are advertising with only has so many in their audience and in order to gain that size audience's attention, you would have to advertise multiple times. Rather than investing in someone who will provide ongoing methods to keep you visible (a publicist), the money spent on advertising is gone after its one-time use.

Another difference between advertising and PR is placement. It is always a plus if you have a full-page, color ad that is prominently placed where your audience can find it. Many times ads are lumped together with other ads in places that viewers may overlook. Commercials are hit or miss because you may or may not be in the car or in front of the television when it airs. Unless you have a first-half Super Bowl commercial that everyone is anticipating, there is just no guarantee that the right person for you will see your advertising campaign. With PR, not only has your story, issue, or product been pitched to a media outlet with an audience that you are sure is your audience, it will be placed in an area where people are looking to read about you. Be it a prominently placed front page editorial, a noon or evening news story that is teased several times before it airs, or a blog with preview tweets, PR pros make sure that your story will be a positive one that will receive ample, recurring circulation to viewers.

Now I know how this sounds and I know what you are thinking: "she is a publicist, of course she prefers PR over advertising" Well you're right. I am a publicist and I do prefer saving my clients money and ensuring the farthest reach for their story, but PR is truly vital to your survival as a business.

Business leader and co-founder of Microsoft, Bill Gates once said, *"If I was down to my last dollar, I would spend it on PR."* That's a pretty big statement. First of all it shows that a business leader as successful as Mr. Gates recognizes how truly valuable public relations is to a company. It could also be a testament to exactly how much of a role public relations played in the success of Microsoft. He understood in this statement that spending that last dollar on PR will yield exponential results for his business; and ultimately profits will increase. Don't get me wrong, there is definitely a place and a need for advertising, but I feel that more importantly, the concepts, identity and strategies that PR evokes are the precedent.

Even if you do not have an ongoing contract with a publicist or PR firm, you should definitely seek these services even if just on a temporary basis. See the following examples:

- The launch of a product or event
- Strategic planning of a new business
- Rebranding efforts
- Publicity to launch you to the next level
- Media Relations
- Relationship building
- Consultations

Any of these areas can happen on a consultation or short-term basis; but I highly recommend that you seek sound counsel from a PR expert, even if it's just to develop a plan that you will implement. My equation is this PR=Success=More PR.

As I mentioned, there is a place and appropriate occasion for advertising. By no means am I trying to deter anyone from purchasing a commercial spot or buying an ad in a magazine. I just want you to understand that doing so does not take the place of PR. Advertising can be used to enhance your efforts and ignite a further reach to your audience, but unless you have a ridiculous amount set aside in your advertising budget, you may want to look at more effective ways to attract your audience.

Now on to marketing, which is the umbrella under which advertising falls. We have stumbled across another blurred line here, but marketing and public relations are definitely counterparts. Marketing is the research and practices involved in the production and purchasing of a product or service. It focuses on demographics, such as who needs your product, what they look like, what they enjoy, average income, what locations your product works best in, driving revenue, paid advertisement. Marketing and PR are counterparts because through marketing research, the public relations strategies can be developed.

Here's an example. Imagine that you are developing a brand for your particular product. In order to tailor your message, you must identify your target audience for that product; that's PR. Now let's say that your target audience is the stay-at-home mom. Marketing research helps you understand everything that there is to know about stay-at-home moms, such as:

- What do they like;
- What's their average age;
- How many children do they have;
- What's their race/ethnicity;
- What TV shows do they watch; and
- What books do they read?

Of course there are others, but once you use marketing research to gather this information, you are better able to understand your audience. Then you can tailor your product (which should have already happened) to the specifics of your audience and with PR you can tailor your messages to that audience. Typically a lot of marketing research happens throughout the journey, but definitely at the beginning conception phase of developing a product.

I sincerely hope that if you have a product or a service, you have already used marketing to gather the necessary information to make sure that you've tailored your product or service to your audience. If you have not, I recommend that you reach out to a marketing expert to help you with an analysis of your business and identify the specifics that will make your business appropriate for your audience.

Let's move into the conversation about order. Have you ever heard of the old idiom, "Don't put the cart before the horse?" I want to use that saying to illustrate a common mistake that I find with businesses. I know that you understand that PR strategy should be a part of the process from conception throughout the birth of your brand. I have to mention, though that all aspects of PR are not necessary to implement from the beginning, namely media relations.

Too many times have I turned away clients because they wanted me to secure media interviews for them when their businesses were not ready to "go public." What I mean is that it's called strategy for a reason. You have to be strategic with media interviews. There are so many variables that come into play before a news director accepts a publicist's media request:

- Relevance
- The news cycle
- The resume

Yes, as superficial as those last few bullet points sound, they are true. Does this mean that you have to look like a supermodel to secure a media interview? Absolutely not, but it does mean that you have to present yourself and your story a certain way before they will consider you. That's why you have to prepare for media interviews. Let's take a look at what I mean.

1. **Is this relevant:** I am not saying that your product or service is not relevant, but are you at the point in your journey where you have things to show and say that are relevant to a general audience? Here's what I mean. When I work with researchers who contact me about writing a press release about the study they are beginning, I have to let them know that the best thing to do is to

contact me at the end, after they have findings from the study. A media outlet is not going to interview a person who can only discuss that they will one day begin a study about the effectiveness of a certain drug.

What more do you have to say about that other than you are about to start? Nothing; and that's not newsworthy. It would not be relevant information and after hearing your interview a viewer will simply say, "so what." After the study has been completed and has findings; however, there may be a breakthrough discovery that will change the world and that's when we pitch the media. Media outlets want facts and relevant information. They want to be able to keep the interest of their viewers and by announcing that you are about to start something that you won't be able to follow back up on until a year later, is not interesting to an audience.

The other piece is that if you are developing a product or service but you aren't ready to receive clients or customers yet, then why seek media at this point in the process? What will happen is that you may participate in an interview, pique the interest of your audience, gain customer inquiries for your product, only to lose clients due to lack of supply. The world's attention span is very short, so if they don't have your product when they decide that they want it, they lose interest. Have you ever noticed that musicians always do media interview tours on the day of their release or after it has already released? You may find that they start their tours a few days before, but it is usually not much before that. This is because they want you to hear their interview and go out and buy their product immediately.

If Fantasia Barrino's album had not been available on the day that I saw her interview, I can honestly say that I would not have purchased it. But as I mentioned, her interview was so compelling that I wanted to support her, so I immediately grabbed my phone and downloaded her album.   Two weeks, two months, and even worse, two years later, your audience has forgotten your very compelling interview. Your media interviews should be aligned with the launch of your brand. That makes it relevant.

Finally, a huge challenge is that sometimes clients simply need to realize that with sex, drugs, war, and entertainment being the most attractive stories to news outlets, the grand opening of your new flower shop just may not make the six o'clock evening news. We can find an alternative audience for your grand opening, but the national headline news or local affiliate (depending on the area) just won't find that particular story relevant for the newscast. Just because your story is not relevant for certain media right now; however, doesn't mean that something else about your business won't be relevant later down the line.

2. **The News Cycle.** The newsroom is a fickle place. What is breaking news at one moment could be old news by the end of the day. I have worked in three different newsrooms and each one had the same personality, fast paced and easily distracted. Seriously, as a publicist, I have had media

interviews scheduled and canceled all within the same hour because the news interest changed.

This happens quite frequently, but I can recall one time in particular that I received a call one day around 4 p.m. from a national network news show that wanted to speak with my client for a live show at 6 p.m. that day. My client was on a flight at the time I received the call, so it wasn't until about an hour later that I could actually speak with him about the interview. The good news was that he was in the city of the news station's headquarters and could easily head over to their studio for the interview.

We were able to arrange and confirm all of this by 5:30 p.m. At the time my client was being interviewed as an expert on a breaking news story. Around 6 p.m., I received a call from the news station that they had other breaking news and had to cancel the interview. Just like that, the entire hour and a half of planning was out the window. The news cycle is unpredictable and doesn't last very long. After about 48 hours on a major story and less than that on a smaller topic, the interest is gone. It's important to note that if your brand is relevant to what is happening in the news, you or your publicist must act quickly to capitalize on the opportunity. It's important to understand; however, that if there is a major news topic happening locally or nationally, your flower shop opening may not even be considered at that time. That's why I highly recommend that when you come to the point of your branding journey when you are ready for media opportunities, do not "try this at home." Talk to a professional and seek their services to make sure that you are able to utilize the gift of the media in the best possible way.

3. **Your Resume.** I could honestly go on and on about this topic, but the last point I feel is worth mentioning is you! The media outlets are checking you out before they commit to conducting your interview. How do I know? Because they are giving me, the publicist, the interrogation. This is yet another reason why you should be aware of your value and achievements.

My job is to emphasize to the media why your story should be told. After we have outlined all of your experiences and accomplishments, I am able to hand your pitch over to the media on a silver platter.

Media outlets always want their newscasts or stories viewed in the best way possible. They want the best subject matter, the best interviews, the most accurate information and the most relevant stories. Your credentials and qualifications must be presented in a way they are comfortable that you will add value to their newscast or magazine. When I pitch my clients to new sources, they want to know if the client has done media before and how they are relevant to the industry at hand. Major market networks also ask for video or story clips of the client's past interviews. This is never a problem because before I pitch my clients, I make sure that they are ready, but it can be an issue if you are not prepared.

Listen to your next local newscast and count how many times the person being interviewed is referred to as an expert. It's because they want the viewers to trust that the information they are hearing is coming from someone knowledgeable and experienced. Let me just add that the subjects are referred to as experts because they are. The expert, in some right, is knowledgeable of the topic that they are discussing. They sound knowledgeable, and they look comfortable discussing their content.

Before you every step in front of a news camera or talk to a reporter of any kind, make sure that you are prepared. Preparation involves...

- **Familiarity with the topic** - even if the interview topic is specifically regarding you or your brand, you must still prepare. The reporter may ask you a few unexpected questions, or you may not recall even the simplest question. Lights, cameras, and microphones are intimidating as well as nerve-wracking even for the most seasoned media mogul. Nervousness is natural and happens to everyone but it can also cause you to forget even the simplest facts about yourself. The best way to help overcome that issue is to review statistics about your brand, or review the history of your brand, and make sure that you are completely familiar with the general topic of your interview.

Familiarity with the reporter or media outlet - this is always a necessity. I never accept an interview for my clients until I know specifics about the media outlet that is requesting the interview. This is important because you do not want to walk into an interview and get blindsided. Say for instance you are an advocate for your interview topic; the reporter or media outline may not support your topic and use your interview as an opportunity to bash your views. There may be a call-in segment where you will need to answer the questions of the general public. You would definitely need to be prepared for that, or it could be an outlet that is not very experienced and depends on you to guide the interview along. That's not necessarily a bad alternative, but it is definitely something that you need to be prepared for.

Three questions that I always ask a reporter before considering an interview are:

- o Is this a live interview?
- o What is the tone of the story?
- o Will there be anyone else interviewed on this topic?

The answers to these three questions are determining factors as to whether or not my client will participate in an interview. Remember that as your brand grows you will not only be proactive in your media outreach, you will also be reactive, meaning that the reporters may begin requesting you without a pitch. That's a great sign of growth, but again it requires preparation. Don't worry; it is definitely achievable.

- **Identifying your key points ahead of time** – This one is similar to what I mentioned earlier about being familiar with your topic. You want to make sure that you not only are familiar with your subject matter but that you also have been thoughtful about your key message for the interview. You are doing this interview for a reason, whether the launch of a book or product; the pre-interview for an upcoming event, or a feature on you, the personal brand. Whatever the case may be, ask yourself what it is you want the audience, not the reporter, but your audience to take away from your interview. Whatever the answer, that's the key message. You then outline a few key points to emphasis that message.

Listen carefully; **Do not write a script that you will try to memorize** for the interview. That is a no-no. When I say to be prepared, I mean think about it, talk it through with your publicist or others and let the information become second nature. By no means should you memorize anything for an interview. That is interview suicide. You will be sure to forget a word that will throw everything else off and you will wind up looking uninformed about your topic. You also lose the natural look. Viewers want to feel like you are having a conversation directly with them. **A rehearsed script sounds untrustworthy; it looks uncomfortable and it is definitely unconvincing.** Practice your interview in the mirror or in front of people; the more you outline your key points, the more familiar you become and the more successful you will be.

Media training with a publicist will help tackle these and other facets of the interview process. The main thing to remember is that you want to portray your brand and capture your key messages in the most favorable light. To do this is not hard, but it does require preparation and practice.

My goal is for my clients to understand that while mass media is important and publicity is necessary, it's not something to jump into without being prepared. This section on PR and media relations comes at the end of the book by design. All of the steps that we've discussed throughout this book must happen before the media aspect is incorporated.

You also don't have to tackle this alone. A publicist can help you turn what seems like a non-relevant story into positive media coverage for your brand by adding the right ingredients to the recipe. Whether you are getting prepared with the right key messages for your interview or prepared by ensuring that you are equipped with the large demand for your product after your interview, lack of strategy in media relations can do more harm than good and remember, the entire concept of public relations is to develop and protect your brand.

I realize that on social media, movies and television shows the red carpet, high profile events, and celebrity endorsements seem appealing and tantalizing. Those aspects will come, but first comes strategic planning, researching, trial and error, and sleepless nights. Trust me when I tell you that it will not take long to see the fruits of your labor. Work hard now, master these branding tactics and see if you won't have increased visibility, effective communication, and a sustainable brand.

Conclusion: **Let's get started**

As we conclude, let me say once again, "Congratulations, It's a Brand!" You've come a long way and now you will travel even further down the road to success. The tools that we've discussed are designed to help you think differently about what your brand will become. These tools are designed to challenge you to think outside of the box and really fine tune your ideas so that you will not only start your business; you will sustain. Now all that's left is for you to do the work.

The mere fact that you are reading this book shows that you have a passion to learn more about the growth and expansion of your brand. You've taken the first step, now keep moving forward. So many times people will have wonderful and very innovative ideas but for various reasons, they never make the move to get started on those ideas. What could have been a multi-million-dollar corporation for someone is still just an idea sitting in their thoughts waiting to be birthed. I said before that you control when you give birth and that's true, but just make sure that you deliver.

How do I get started? What do I do next? How will I know? All of these questions have been asked of me when I provide consultations with people about their business. My answer is very simple. "Just get started." The longer you wait, the longer we, your potential clients and customers have to wait. There is a need for your business. Don't make those who need you wait any longer, simply because you are intimidated by the work that is required.

When an idea hits you, act on it. This doesn't mean that you have an idea for a business today and then tomorrow you are open for business, but it does mean that you can have an idea today and start researching it today. You may have an idea about a partnership with a corporation or company today, if so, start looking up contacts and make the calls to connect with those companies. I have found that when I hurry and act on an idea, it forces me to actually go through with it. I'm held accountable because I've already made the first moves.

I do want you to think about what you are doing and not act hastily. Thinking is an action; so even if you have an idea, thinking on it more is still a form of getting started. My only request is that you don't just waste perfectly good ideas. Also don't get overwhelmed, there are people and services available that can guide you through the process so that it seems less intimidating. Utilize those resources, do whatever it takes to make you a better businessperson and act accordingly to build a better brand.

As parents we have to trust our judgment and our instincts. Yes, we will make mistakes and not all decisions will be the best decisions, but I really believe that there is a special quality in a leader that automatically equips us with the ability to bounce back. Parents of both children and brands make mistakes often, but we adjust, regroup, and build and most importantly, learn from those mistakes so that the next attempt will be great.

Again, trust is key. You want your brand to be trustworthy and you have to be willing to trust the process and be patient as you endure the process.

Branding is imperative for business success and public relations is imperative to developing the most effective tactics to communicate the messages of your brand. At the end of the day, you want a consistent brand that your clients can connect with. The lists, the plans, the questions, and all of the strategic development tactics are tedious and extremely thought provoking; but once you find the answers, you will be amazed at how perfectly all of the other pieces connect to the branding and PR puzzle.